The Scientific Proof of God

Unified Field Theory Revealed

A Holistic Model of Physics,
Integrating the Dimensions of Consciousness
and Intention into the Standard Model of Physics

Fredrick Swaroop Honig

The Scientific Proof of God

Unified Field Theory Revealed

A Holistic Model of Physics, Integrating the Dimensions of Consciousness and Intention into the Standard Model of Physics.

First Edition.

© Copyright 2017 by Spirit of Aloha Temple Inc.

Published
Aviva Publishing
Lake Placid, NY
www.AvivaPubs.com

Editor

Tyler R. Tichelaar, Ph.D.
Superior Book Productions

Design and Layout: Larry Alexander, M.A.

ISBN: 9781944335670

Library of Congress: 2017903935

Address all inquiries to: Spirit of Aloha Temple Inc.

Email: Info@SpiritofAloha.org

Website: www.SpiritofAloha.org

Dedication

The All Faiths Yantra® was designed by Sri Swami Satchidananda as a universal symbol of unity and a reminder that there are many paths to the one Source.[1]

1 By permission of Satchidananda Ashram – Yogaville, Inc. *www.Yogaville.Org*

THIS BOOK IS dedicated to people of all faiths who yearn to live in harmony with nature by understanding and aligning with the Unitive Consciousness pervading the universe. It is also dedicated to those who have nurtured my growth and my service; principal among these are the following:

My parents, Jean and Jacob Honig, whose open-mindedness encouraged me to follow my dreams and whose generosity helped to fund them.

My siblings, Jiya, Robert, Edward, and Angel, who have inspired and supported me along my path.

My grandmother's cousin, physicist Lise Meitner, whose life, courage, and discovery of nuclear fission have been a lifelong inspiration for me. This book is dedicated as a continuation of her legacy.

Swami Satchidananda and Swami Swaroopanda
(Fredrick Swaroop Honig)

My Guru, Sri Swami Satchidananda, and his spiritual sangha, who offered me a nurturing environment and guidance for my growth and service.

My Guru's Guru, Sri Swami Sivananda, whose life and books express the essence of Unitive Consciousness.

The University of California at Berkeley where I was encouraged to think for myself and to nurture my love of science.

My many friends who generously contribute to my joy, growth, and mission.

I offer my sincere gratitude to the Unitive Field for manifesting in my life this loving, dynamic, and supportive team. I trust that the inspirations that I have received from them are shared in this book.

Acknowledgments

I OFFER MY deepest gratitude for inspiration and guidance in the writing of this book to the following:

Spirit of Aloha Botanical Gardens and Bird Sanctuary

For the past 24 years, I have served as the Nature Guardian of The Spirit of Aloha Botanical Gardens and Bird Sanctuary. The Gardens is a sacred eleven-acre oceanfront Hawaiian historical site. It is a living cell of heaven, and a template for living in harmony with nature. While I have been building its structures and gardens, it has been strengthening my character and opening me to a deeper understanding and trust in the benevolence of the Unitive Field expressing itself as nature.
www.TheGardens.Org

My mother Jean Honig was my first Guru and lifelong mentor. At age eighty-nine, she wrote a brilliant book just months before her sacred spiritual transition entitled *Gems from a Magic Jeanie*. This book encapsulates Unitive wisdom. www.TheGardens.Org/JeanHonig

My sister Jiya Kowarsky has been my wisdom guide since my childhood. Her latest book, *River of Joy*, contains Unitive wisdom through inspirational poems. This wisdom is a foundation of Unitive Field Theory. Jiya also graciously guided me in the editing of this book to help make it flow and be enjoyable to read like her poems. *www.amazon.com/River-Joy-Jiya/dp/059542306X*

My sister Meenakshi Angel Honig who, at a very young age and because of her compassion for animals, became a vegetarian. She helped to move our whole family to embrace plant-based nutrition. Her newest book, *Feel Good Now*, offers a comprehensive understanding of Vegan nutrition and is a pillar of Unitive Field Theory. *www.AngelYoga.com*

Mr. Merman, my 5th Grade Science Teacher at Colfax school in Pittsburgh, who offered an after school science club where I wired and assembled my first electric motor and discovered that science was fun.

My editor Tyler R. Tichelaar, Ph.D., for his genius with words in helping me to craft scientific concepts into language that is easy to understand. Tyler is also a brilliant novelist who re-imagines history in life-affirming ways. *www.MarquetteFiction.com*

Dr. Paul Prasant Hansma, Physics Professor Emeritus, University of California, Santa Barbara is a member of The Spirit of Aloha Temple Advisory Board. He has supported me with my projects for over thirty years. Dr. Hansma is one of the most acclaimed scientists of our era and an inventor of the first atomic force microscope to image samples in fluid. He is now developing the first technology capable of measuring human bone strength. Prasant is an inspirational model to me, a person who balances the life of a scientist with the deepest wisdom of spirituality. It is that balance that is the essence of Unitive Field Theory. *http://hansmalab.physics.ucsb.edu*

Swami Swaroopananda (Fredrick Swaroop Honig)
and Dr. Prasant Hansma worked together with
Swami Satchidananda on the design, engineering, and installation of
The Light of Truth Universal Shrine (LOTUS) altar lights.[2]

Dr. Wayne Dyer was one of the most inspired teachers of our era. His books, lectures, and PBS specials have made him a world leader in the field of consciousness. He has recently made his transition into his next sacred spiritual realm.

Wayne was a friend, colleague, and member of our non-profit service organization, The Spirit of Aloha Temple's Advisory Board. Over the past twenty years, he visited The Gardens many times with his family and gave me inscribed copies of his books. In 2004, he gave me his newest masterpiece, *The Power of Intention*.

In this book, Wayne insightfully describes the force of intention as an integral organizing principle of the universe. Inspirations from his book are incorporated into Unitive Field Theory and are part of Wayne's enduring legacy. *www.drwaynedyer.com*

Dr. Wayne Dyer, Dr. Richard Alpert (Ram Dass)
Fredrick Swaroop Honig

Swaroop,
It is such a genuine pleasure to be on this planet with you as colleagues.
All Love and Light,
Wayne Dyer, Maui, 25 July 04

Contents

Foreword

The Unitive Field

T IS MY honor to share in these pages my understandings of the Unitive
Field. At heart, I am a scientist who sees nature as a Unitive Field of
Consciousness. My life is the expression of my service to nature. I have
had the good fortune to study with great leaders in the science of physics
as well as in the science of consciousness.

It is on their shoulders that I stand. This book aims to incorporate both sciences into one integrated science that strengthens them both. The ideas presented in this book as Unitive Field Theory are based on my understanding of nature and physics, as well as intuitive wisdom and inspirations I have had about them.

Here is an important quote from Albert Einstein to help in understanding Unitive Field Theory: "The intellect has little to do on the road to discovery. There comes a leap in consciousness, call it intuition or what you will, the solution comes to you and you don't know how or why... the truly valuable thing is intuition."

The Unitive Field is the Matrix of Matter

The sciences of consciousness and physics are complementary and their union is Unitive Field Theory. Unitive Field Theory addresses the twelve fundamental questions that remain unanswered in the current standard model of physics. Each chapter that follows offers deep insights into one of these questions. When finished, readers should have a better understanding of nature and their connection to the Unitive Consciousness that pervades the universe.

The Six layers of the ego that like storm clouds hide humanity's perception of Unitive Consciousness

In the world today, six main mental delusions exist that cloud humanity's perception of Unitive Consciousness.

They are as follows:

1. **Racial Egoism**: This delusion states, "Members of other races are lower on the scale of evolution than members of my race; therefore, practicing the Golden Rule does not apply to them. They can be exploited for the benefit of our race."

2. **National Egoism**: Under the banner of patriotism, this harmful dogma promotes, "My country is the greatest country; therefore, it has the inherent right to exploit other countries to maintain its superiority." This mindset ignores the Golden Rule when it comes to dealing with other countries. This belief is another main cause of the suffering that exists in the world today.

3. **Religious Egoism**: This intolerant philosophy teaches, "My religion is the only true religion; all other religions are false religions." It denies the rights of others to understand God in their own unique

ways. This philosophy creates a horrible mental plague, which is a principle cause of the wars and violence we see in the world today.

4. **Human Species Egoism**: This delusional philosophy states that humanity has the right to exploit nature in ways that benefit humanity but are harmful to nature and other species. It ignores the Golden Rule when dealing with nature or other species. This mental delusion is the main cause of the worldwide devastation of nature and the mass extinctions we are experiencing today.

5. **Spiritual Egoism**: This materialistic philosophy ignores the role that the Unitive consciousness plays as an organizing force in the universe. Instead, it proposes that the universe is random, without intention, and came into being through an uncontrolled explosion. This ignores the laws of physics by assuming that there is an effect without a cause, a highly ordered universe without an organizing principle. Unsuccessfully, those deluded by this erroneous mindset attempt to fill their spiritual void with an excess of material possessions or by trying to obtain power and prestige. This generates a life experience that is competitive instead of cooperative, cruel instead of compassionate, and disconnected instead of Unitive.

6. **Individual Egoism**: This delusion asserts that my own importance and welfare is more important than that of others. It influences the mind to commit actions perceived to be needed to be happy even at the expense of the welfare of others. It ignores the Golden Rule in the name of trying to satisfy the mind's insatiable demands. It makes those infected with its influence slaves of their own minds and robs them of the peace and true freedom that comes from the mastery of one's own mind.

Within the following twelve chapters is presented the scientific proof for the existence of God, a Unitive Consciousness pervading the universe and an ecumenical understanding for personally experiencing it in your daily life.

Introduction

THE **U**NITIVE **F**IELD Integrates the Science of Physics with the Science of Consciousness.

Physics is a science that seeks to explain how the universe works. The current standard model of physics is incomplete and unable to address nature's fundamental qualities of consciousness and intention. Unitive Field Theory addresses the twelve fundamental questions that remain unanswered in the standard model of physics. In this book, we will explore those twelve fundamental questions.

Before we begin, however, let's look at how Unitive Field Theory has a foundation in the beliefs of three well-known scientists—Albert Einstein, Lise Meitner, and Isaac Newton. I'll present a short description of how each scientist offers unique insights into the understanding of Unitive Field Theory and then some quotations from them that support this theory.

Albert Einstein (14 March 1879 – 18 April 1955)
during a lecture in Vienna[3]

Albert Einstein spent the second half of his life searching for one theory that would explain all the laws of physics. Intuitively, he believed that all of nature's laws would be explained by one fundamental law that he called Unified Field Theory.

I believe Einstein had already discovered his Unified Field Theory, but he was not able to apply it to the standard model of physics because the standard model of physics was itself lacking in its understanding of nature. The standard model of physics does not take into account the force that is the very foundation of the universe—Consciousness and its force of Intention.

---

3   Photo: https://commons.wikimedia.org/wiki/File:Einstein_1921_by_F_Schmutzer.jpg

Once the dimension of Consciousness and the dimension of Intention are added into the standard model of physics, Einstein's Theory of Relativity, $E=mc^2$, is the one equation that explains the causation of the universe. For when Relativity is applied to the dimensions of Consciousness and Intention, it becomes the Unitive Field Theory of Causation.

This theory explains in one equation how the one Consciousness of the universe manifested the mass and energy needed to build the universe. This equation also explains the relationship between the cause and effect of any action. The Theory of Relativity applied to the dimensions of Consciousness and Intention form the missing links that complete Einstein's Unified Field Theory.

I have chosen to call this Unitive Field Theory instead of Unified Field Theory because the field has always been One or Unitive; it has never been separated and, therefore, has never needed to be put together or unified.

Quotes by Albert Einstein that are foundational to Unitive Field Theory:

1. "Science can only be created by those who are thoroughly imbued with the aspiration toward truth and understanding. This source of feeling, however, springs from the sphere of religion.... The situation may be expressed by an image: science without religion is lame, religion without science is blind."[4]

2. "My religiosity consists of a humble admiration of the infinitely superior spirit that reveals itself in the little we are able to perceive of reality with our frail and feeble mind."[5]

3. "A human being is a part of a whole, called by us universe, a part limited in time and space. He experiences himself, his thoughts and feelings as something separated from the rest...a kind of optical delusion of his consciousness. This delusion is a kind of a prison for us, restricting us to our personal desires and to affection for a few persons nearest to us. Our task must be to free ourselves from this prison by widening our circle of compassion to embrace all living creatures and the whole of nature in its beauty."[6]

---

4 Science, Philosophy, and Religion: A Symposium, 1941

5 From a letter to M.M. Schayer, August 1927

6 Condolence letter to Normal Salit, March 4, 1950

4. "Nothing will benefit human health and increase the chances for survival of life on Earth as much as the evolution to a vegetarian diet.... Vegetarian food leaves a deep impression on our nature. If the whole world adopts vegetarianism, it can change the destiny of humankind."[7]

5. "I want to know how God created this world. I am not interested in this or that phenomenon, in the spectrum of this or that element. I want to know his thoughts. The rest are details."[8]

6. "Look deep into nature, and then you will understand everything better."[9]

7. "Although I am a typical loner in daily life, my consciousness of belonging to the invisible community of those who strive for truth, beauty, and justice keeps me from feeling isolated. The most beautiful and deepest experience a man can have is the sense of the mysterious. It is the underlying principle of religion as well as of all serious endeavour in art and science. He who never had this experience seems to me, if not dead, then at least blind. To sense that behind anything that can be experienced there is a something that our minds cannot grasp, whose beauty and sublimity reaches us only indirectly: this is religiousness. In this sense I am religious. To me it suffices to wonder at these secrets and to attempt humbly to grasp with my mind a mere image of the lofty structure of all there is."[10]

8. "Only a life lived for others is a life worthwhile."[11]

[12]

Albert Einstein

---

7 A popular quotation attributed to Albert Einstein whose source is unknown

8 "Talk with Einstein" (Listener 54, 1955) Esther Salama

9 "To Margot Einstein, after his sister's Maja's death, 1951; quote by Hanna Loewy in A&E Television Einstein Biography, VPI International, 1991

10 From "My Credo" Autumn 1932

11 Quote to *The New York Times*, June 20, 1932. AEA 29-041

12 Einstein's signature: https://commons.wikimedia.org/wiki/File: Albert_Einstein_ signature_1934.svg

Lise Meitner (7 November 1878 – 27 October 1968)

Fredrick Swaroop Honig is one of the few
living members of Lise Meitner's family.
Lise Meitner was his grandmother's cousin.

Few humans have had the courage to follow their dreams as did Lise Meitner. She nurtured her love of science at a time when universities in Europe would not admit women as students or faculty. She pioneered the rights of women in science and was the first woman to become a professor of physics in Germany. Albert Einstein called her "The Marie Curie of Germany."

Lise Meitner was the visionary whose brilliance allowed her to be the first person to understand and explain nuclear fission. It was she who named this process "fission." She opened the door to the nuclear age. She was a pacifist whose life expressed non-violence. She worked solely on the peaceful applications of nuclear energy. Her legacy is a cornerstone of Unified Field Theory.

Lise Meitner was born in Austria of Jewish descent and, like Einstein, had to escape from the fascist regime in Germany during World War II. She continued her research in Sweden where she and her nephew, Otto Frisch, were the first to explain the process of nuclear fission.

"At a secret meeting in 1938, Meitner urged Otto Hahn and his laboratory partner Fritz Strassman to perform additional tests on neutron-bombarded uranium. Hahn and Strassman finally determined that the

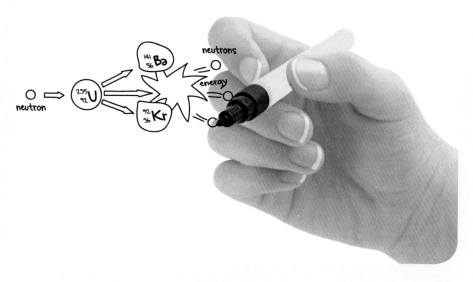

Nuclear Fission

end result included the much lighter element barium, not the expected heavy element radium. This was very puzzling. Hahn recognized that uranium atoms completely breaking apart into much smaller atoms would be an explanation, but how could that happen?

Hahn wrote to Meitner: "Perhaps you can come up with some sort of fantastic explanation. We knew ourselves that [uranium] can't actually burst apart into [barium]."

Meitner and her nephew, Otto Frisch, while outdoors skiing, realized Bohr's "liquid-drop" model of the atomic nucleus could explain the result mathematically. Frisch described the moment as follows: "We [Frisch and Lise Meitner] walked up and down in the snow, I on skis and she on foot (she said and proved that she could get along just as fast that way), and gradually the idea took shape that this was no chipping or cracking of the nucleus but rather a process to be explained by Bohr's idea that the nucleus was like a liquid drop; such a drop might elongate and divide itself."[13,14]

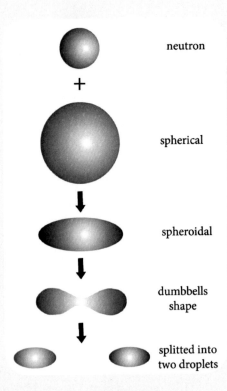

neutron

spherical

spheroidal

dumbbells shape

splitted into two droplets

---

13 Otto Frisch and John A. Wheeler, "The Discovery of Fission," *Physics Today*, Nov 1967, 20, 47.

14 Also recommended: *Lise Meitner and the Dawn of the Nuclear Age*, by Patricia Rife, www.amazon.com/Lise-Meitner-Dawn-Nuclear-Age/dp0817645594

They scribbled formulas on a scrap of paper in the woods: A uranium atom could elongate when bombarded by neutrons, and occasionally, some of the uranium atoms could split apart into two "smaller drops." In fact, the uranium atoms in Hahn's experiments had split to form the much lighter atoms barium and krypton, and they had ejected neutrons and a very large amount of energy, with a loss of some mass. Meitner was the first to realize Einstein's famous equation $E=mc^2$ was at play here, converting mass into energy."

Lise Meitner was actually a member of my family; she was my maternal grandmother's cousin. I had the great fortune of being raised in the same tradition as she was— namely, being encouraged to "Listen to your parents but think for yourself."

Lise Meitner is a scientist whose courage and insights are fundamental to Unitive Field Theory.

Quotes by Lise Meitner that are foundational to Unitive Field Theory:

1. "As children, we were taught to listen to our parents, but to think for ourselves."

2. "Life need not be easy, provided only that it is not empty."

3. "You must not blame us scientists for the use with which war technicians have put our discoveries."

4. "Science makes people reach selflessly for truth and objectivity; it teaches people to accept reality, with wonder and admiration, not to mention the deep awe and joy that the natural order of things brings to the true scientist."

[15]

---

15 https://commons.wikimedia.org/wiki/File:Lise_Meitner_signature.svg

Isaac Newton
(25 December 1642 – 20 March 1727)

Isaac Newton is the father of modern physics. His wisdom is a cornerstone of human culture and science. He owned over forty editions of the Bible and studied them as carefully as he studied the laws of physics. In his life, he incorporated the wisdom of spirituality with the wisdom of science. He is a guiding light for all who strive to understand the true nature of the universe.

Quotes by Isaac Newton that are foundational to Unitive Field Theory:

1. "If I have seen further it is by standing on the shoulders of Giants."

2. "Tact is the knack of making a point without making an enemy."

3. "Men build too many walls and not enough bridges."

4. "What we know is a drop, what we don't know is an ocean."

5. "What goes up must come down…. Gravity explains the motions of the planets, but it cannot explain who sets the planets in motion."

6. "Truth is ever to be found in the simplicity, and not in the multiplicity and confusion of things."

7. "This most beautiful system of the sun, planets and comets, could only proceed from the counsel and dominion of an intelligent and powerful Being."

[16]

---

16 Newton signature: https://en.wikipedia.org/wiki/Isaac_Newton
https://en.wikipedia.org/wiki/Isaac_Newton#/media/File:GodfreyKneller-Isaac-Newton-1689.jpg

Inscription given to Swaroopananda by Swami Satchidananda
in 1996

Chapter 1:
How Many Dimensions Exist in the Universe?

The Universe's Primal Singularity Double Tetrahedron

UNDERSTANDING THE UNIVERSE helps us to understand ourselves.

The application of Einstein's understanding, "Look deep into nature, and then you will understand everything better," provides us with a guide to an understanding of Unitive Field Theory and its goal. In a way, the universe is the mirror that we use to see ourselves. Most scriptures say that man is made in the image of God. So by knowing God or nature, we come to know ourselves. If we look closely at nature, we will see that it is based on selfless service.

Everything in nature is serving its function to help the whole machinery of the universe function smoothly. The goal behind life is to help perpetuate the diversity of species, each of which provides a vital link in the chain of life.

In order for us to understand ourselves or understand the nature of the universe, we have to understand the fundamental essence of creation, which is consciousness.

Consciousness is, in fact, a dimension of the universe. The universe could not exist without it. It is the organizing principle for the universe's manifestation.

Everything in the universe has consciousness, whether it is a life form or just an atom.

Every part of nature obeys the laws of nature precisely. That ability to follow nature's laws is the proof of everything's consciousness.

Humans are designed by nature to be the guardians of nature's diversity. We are given intellectual and physical skills needed for this purpose. We are also given a clear conscience that can discern what is appropriate action.

If we fulfill our mission and protect nature and its biodiversity, our conscience grows and our intellect flowers, and we attain a state of peace called Unitive Consciousness.

In this state, we vibrate in harmony with the Unitive Consciousness that pervades the universe, and because of that resonance, we are effortlessly able to download universal wisdom.

To obtain, live, and flourish because of that wisdom is the goal of the experience we call life.

The Universe is one living organism; therefore, our individuality is a burden we do not need to carry. If we choose, we can align with Unitive Consciousness and allow its energy to flow through us.

When its energy does flow through us, we have reached the state known as "enlightenment."

However, it should be noted that even in this state, it is necessary for the mind to be grateful for the joy that is given in the daily experience of life and to let go of the notion of perfect bliss.

Perfect bliss does not exist, and its expectation is a fallacy that can keep us from experiencing the here and now joy of life.

In order to experience Unitive Consciousness, a type of surrender to accepting the realities of life is needed. Within this realm of life on earth, here and now is the possibility of living in peace and ease and in dynamic service. To achieve this possibility, the desire to be serviceful without demanding a certain outcome is needed. We have to do our best and leave the rest. And when we do that, we find that Unitive energy flows through us and we are free from the burden of our lives.

Consciousness is the first dimension of the Universe. Consciousness is expressed in nature as the full spectrum of electromagnetic waves. This includes radio waves, microwaves, infrared waves, visible light, ultraviolet light, x-rays, and gamma rays, all of which travel at the speed of light. These electromagnetic waves are all an expression of the Universe's dimension of consciousness.

All life forms emit electromagnetic waves that can be detected and photographed. All matter and all energy emit electromagnetic waves.

The Unitive Consciousness is aware in every moment of all electromagnetic waves within the universe. Ultimately, the human brain is a microcosm of the Unitive Consciousness. It also functions with electromagnetic energy. The predominant color vibration for the universe's dimension of consciousness is violet, the light wave with the highest vibration of visible light.

All electromagnetic waves induce a magnetic field by their movement. These magnetic fields form the universe's second dimension of Intention. This dimension is the muscle of the universe that converts the consciousness into action. It is animated by the Law of Causal Intention that will be described in Chapter 3. The predominant color vibration for the universe's dimension of intention corresponds to the light spectrum for the color blue, which is the second highest energy of visible light.

The remaining four dimensions of the universe—Time and the three dimensions of Space—are the same as those described in the standard model of physics.

1. Consciousness (o)	Violet
2. Intention (i)	Blue
3. Time (t)	Green
4. Lateral (x)	Yellow
5. Longitudinal (y)	Orange
6. Vertical dimension (z)	Red

According to Unitive Field Theory, the universe exists in six dimensions. Each dimension represents one of the colors of the visible light spectrum:

The Universe exists in six dimensions,
each with a corresponding light spectrum

By incorporating the dimensions of Consciousness and Intention into the standard model of physics, we acknowledge the wisdom that is the basis of the Universe. This acknowledgment opens us up to experience this wisdom in our daily lives, and it frees us from the illusion of separateness. It is the key to freedom and fulfillment. All lovers of truth should have the humility to understand that the universe itself is one living organism that is, ultimately, our deepest reality.

The Earth is a cell within the body of the living Universe.

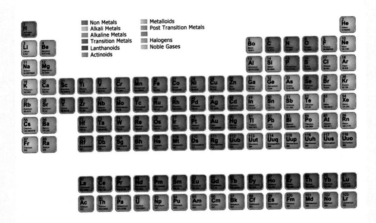

The Periodic Table of Elements
demonstrates the precision and order of the
Unitive Consciousness that is the foundation of the universe.

Element 99 with symbol Es was named Einsteinium in honor
of Albert Einstein.

Element 109 with symbol Mt was named Meitnerium in honor
of Lise Meitner.

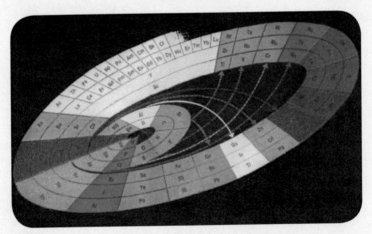

The Fingerprint of God

The Periodic Table aligns perfectly in a Fibonacci spiral.[17]

17 https://en.wikipedia.org/wiki/File:ChemicalGalaxy_Longman_1951.jpg#file

Chapter 2:
What Is the Nature of Consciousness, and How Did It Arise?

I**N THE STANDARD** model of physics, the question of consciousness is considered to be "The Hard Problem."[18]

The reason it is "The Hard Problem" is that we are the consciousness itself, and, therefore, a subject can never see itself directly. To make this clear, think of it as similar to how we cannot actually see our own face; rather, we can see its reflection or its image.

Our eternal identity is pure consciousness. We can never actually experience our own consciousness directly, for a subject cannot become an object. For a subject to see itself, it needs a mirror. Our mirror is that which we call the mind.

When the mind is still and calm, it reflects to our consciousness the image of our true nature; then we experience peace, joy, and fulfillment. When the mind is disturbed, it reflects back to our same conscious awareness the experiences of anxiety, confusion, distortion, and depression.

The goal of all spiritual paths is to learn the skill of keeping the mind still and calm so that it reflects back to us our true nature. The goal of life is to learn to keep the mirror clean and steady. Unitive Field Theory is the science that sheds light on the skills needed to maintain a mind that reflects clearly our pure conscious awareness.

---

18 See https://en.wikipedia.org/wiki/Hard_problem_of_consciousness for a thorough explanation of this problem.

It should be noted that even when the mind is disturbed and is reflecting back to the consciousness a disturbed emotion or anxious thought pattern, the consciousness is aware of that disturbance, but on its deepest levels, it is still peacefully watching the disturbed mind. All the mental anguish experienced is only on the superficial levels of consciousness. That is why we clearly know when we are disturbed. If the consciousness were to be totally disturbed, it could not even judge that it was disturbed.

The goal of the experience we call life is to attain the state of Unitive Consciousness; in this state, the individual consciousness resonates with the Unitive Consciousness and experiences its true oneness.

The core of consciousness is a sound vibration called the Nada or the Word. This primordial sacred vibration gives rise to the awareness of "I am," and it is the foundation of the one Unitive Consciousness that is the source of all consciousness in the universe. Consciousness creates intention in the same way electricity passing through a wire creates a magnetic field around the wire. The movement of electricity itself is an expression of the movement of consciousness, and magnetism is an expression of intention.

Integrated into this "I am" consciousness is the intention to know "Who am I?" and "How may I serve?" This intention is the primal causal intention (c_i), which generates first the Unitive Field, then the primal singularity, which is the seed of the universe. This seed expands into the observable universe with its abundant thriving life forms.

In the universe, there exists only one Unitive Consciousness. All conscious awareness in the universe is one with Unitive Consciousness. If one is experiencing consciousness, that consciousness is eternal and united with Unitive Consciousness. The content of the experience for any being is constantly changing. The consciousness is aware of these changes, yet it never changes. It is the screen upon which the movie of awareness is projected. It is unaffected by the movie just as a screen does not change its properties because of the movie being projected onto it. All awareness is eternally one with Unitive Consciousness. The universe is one eternal consciousness perceiving itself through many windows.

The universe's first dimension of consciousness depicted in violet
generates the second dimension of intention depicted in blue.

The substratum of the universe is its first dimension of consciousness.
From this first dimension, the other five dimensions are cyclically
projected and then withdrawn back into the first. The universe's first
dimension of consciousness is the underlying reality, energy, and
organizing principle of the six dimensions of the Unitive Field.

In Unitive Field Theory, matter does not create consciousness; rather,
consciousness creates matter.

Matter cannot exist without consciousness. It is consciousness that is
the organizing principle for energy and matter. In the science of pattern
organization, known as cymatics or sacred geometry, it is shown that
the vibration of a note creates geometrical patterns on the surface of
water or loose particles such as sand. Similarly, the Nada vibration of
consciousness organizes the Unitive Field.

The diagram below of the Spiraled Sun is an example of Cymatic patterns
generated by sound vibrations.

When you vibrate a liquid or sand with 432 hertz, you can create Cymatic Patterns of Fibonacci Spirals.

The Unitive Field is a vortex animated by six pairs of foundational qualities. Each quality has an attraction to the next quality in the cycle. This attraction powers the eternal vibration of the sacred Nada or Word. On the quantum level, this rotation is comprised of six pairs of causal intentions (c_i). Each causal intention is attracted to the next causal intention in the sequence, thus generating the rotation of the motor that drives the universe.

These six pairs form the energy vortex depicted in the mandala below. The star represents the rotor of the primal singularity that is rotating at the speed of light. The rotor is powered by the causal force of intention (c_i) and generated by the attraction of each quality to the next in the cyclic progression.

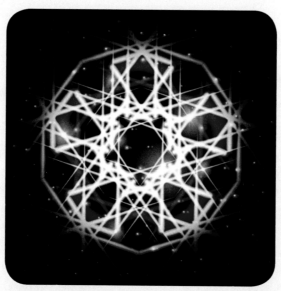

The Primal Singularity six pair causal intention Rotor

In Unitive Field Theory, the universe's first dimension of consciousness is comprised of six pairs of foundational qualities. These are the same qualities at the core of all religions and cultures. The attainment of the first virtue in each pair leads to the attainment of the second virtue. Each virtue is a stepping stone to the next. It all starts with Gratitude, which is a mindset that focuses on appreciating our present moment life experience as a perfect tool for our ultimate growth.

1. Gratitude – Humility
2. Respect – Simplicity
3. Cooperation – Honesty
4. Happiness – Love
5. Service – Freedom
6. Peace – Unity

Each of these foundational qualities is attracted to the next quality in the sequence. This attraction creates a rotation within the primal singularity that generates the causal intention (c_i) for the creation of the Unitive Field itself and then the primal singularity. The singularity is the seed that ultimately gives birth to the universe and its abundant life forms.

The Unitive Field's Theory of Asymmetry, also known as the Theory of Imperfection or the Theory of Dynamic Motion, will be described in more detail in Chapter 9, but for now, it basically means that in all dimensions of the universe, there is a certain amount of randomness or unevenness to ensure that a perfect equilibrium or state of static stability will never exist.

Because of this Theory of Asymmetry, in order for consciousness to exist, there must be a certain differentiation, irregularity, imperfection, or angst. That angst exists in the intention to know "Who am I?" and "How may I serve?" That intention will never be fully realized because as soon as a certain attainment is achieved, the vision of a higher horizon becomes apparent and the intention continues to aspire and evolve into higher and higher realms of life and consciousness. This evolution is, ultimately, the driving force for the evolution of the living universe.

In Unitive Field Theory, it should not be expected that a state of perfect happiness and/or absolute bliss will be experienced. This unrealistic expectation itself creates disturbances in the mind. Even in the state of Unitive Consciousness, there will always be a certain selfless desire that will keep a perfect peace from being achieved. This way, the consciousness is always moving forward and growing, aspiring, and evolving. This is the nature of life and consciousness. If we expect a state of unending bliss, we will be disappointed with our daily experience of life. Instead, we should be grateful for the joy woven into the daily fabric of our life experiences and for the peace that is experienced by a still mind. Unitive Consciousness is a state of mental stillness, during which dynamic service is flowing through us. Our minds are focused, joyful, and at ease. It is an attainable state, which is the goal of the experience that we call life.

Unitive Consciousness resonates with the six pairs of foundational qualities. When our own minds resonate with the same qualities, the state of harmonic resonance occurs and we experience our oneness with Unitive Consciousness.

In this state of oneness, which may also be called yoga, union, enlightenment, or salvation, the feeling of separateness evaporates as the experience of oneness prevails.

To achieve this state of harmonic resonance and oneness is the goal of the study of Unitive Field Theory.

Chapter 3

What Is the Effect of Consciousness and Intention on the Universe, and How Can This Force Be Measured?

The Crab Nebula19 is a nursery for the formation of new stars from the gases released by a previous supermassive star that transformed in a supernova. In this process, heavier elements are formed that are needed for the evolution of life in the universe.

---

19 https://en.wikipedia.org/wiki/Crab_Nebula#/media/File:Crab_Nebula.jpg One of the largest mosaic images ever taken by NASA's Hubble Space Telescope of the Crab Nebula, a six-light-year-wide expanding remnant of a star's supernova explosion.

A T THE ROOT of all religions and all systems of culture is the practice of ethical perfection. This collective wisdom is eloquently summarized in teachings of The Golden Rule: Do unto others as you would have them do unto you.

The reason this rule exists is because what we do unto others will ultimately be done unto us. In other words, "What goes around comes around." It is the Law of Cause and Effect.

Most scriptures also state that if we take one step toward God, God will take ten steps toward us. By extension, therefore, if we took ten steps toward God, God would take 100 steps toward us.

This ratio reflects the square of the effort: $10^2 = 100$. The Unitive Field Theory of Causation agrees with this universal ancient wisdom's equation for describing the cause and effect of any action.

What is the true cause of an action? It is the intention behind the action. All action in every realm of nature has as its actual source a causal intention. Intention is the source of action.

In Unitive Field Theory, the equation for measuring the relationship between the cause and effect of any action is known as the Law of Causal Intention. This equation is the application of the Theory of Relativity, $E=mc^2$, in the universe's first dimension of consciousness and in its second dimension of causal intention.

$$c_i^2\, m = E \quad \textbf{The Unitive Field Law of Causal Intention}$$

c_i = Causal intention of an action

m = Mass affected by the action

E = Energy return to causal intention

This equation defines the relationship between the cause and effect of any action.

Every action in the universe has as its source a causal intention (c_i). That causal intention squared times the mass of those affected by the action (m) equals the energy returned to the causal intention (E).

In other words, the causal intention squared times the mass of those affected by the action equals the energy returned to the source of the causal intention. This theory has been referred to as "The Law of Karma" or "The Golden Rule."

The energy of the Unitive Field is comprised at its most elementary level as a force of intention (c_i) that is measured in a unit of force called the Hreem.

Following are estimations of the magnitudes of the Hreem force's causal intentions (c_i) in the evolutionary progression of life forms.

For example, in the first one, a virus has an intention to live and propagate that is equivalent to .01 Hreem:

The Phylogenetic Tree	Hreem
virus	.01
bacteria	.1
cellular organism	1
multicellular organism	10
plant	100
insect	1,000
fish	10,000
bird	100,000
mammal	1,000,000
human	10,000,000
human practicing non-violence	100,000,000
human established in Unitive consciousness	1,000,000,000
The Unitive Field's causal intention (c_i) to bring forth a universe that nurtures life	10^{144}

The Unitive Field's causal intention of 10^{144} Hreem to bring forth a universe that nurtures life forms is the primal force that organizes all matter and energy in the universe. This force in the standard model of physics is referred to as dark energy. It is the primary organizing force of the Universe. This organizing Hreem energy comprises approximately 72.1 percent of the mass-energy of the universe.

Birds have a desire to live and perpetuate their species with
a force of 100,000 Hreem

Hreem energy is on the larger scales evenly distributed throughout the universe and on the smaller scales appears as the filaments of a sponge in a pattern similar to the distribution of observable mass within the universe.

The Unitive Field's Hreem energy of causal intention (c_i) 10^{144} is eloquently presented in an ancient Vedic Sanskrit sloka (a wisdom verse) that has been meditated upon by yogis for over five millennia.

The sacred Omkaaram Sloka:

> Omkaaram Bindu Samyuktam
> Nityam Dhyaayanti Yoginaha
> Kaamadam Mokshadam Chaiva
> Omkaaraaya Namo Namaha

Word by word translation:

> Omkaaram = the vibration of Om = the Nada =
> the Hreem = the Unitive Field of Consciousness =
> Bindu = the primordial singularity, the Godhead

Samyuktam = totally united with
Nityam = eternally
Dhyaayanti = meditated upon
Yoginaha = by the yogis

Kaamadam = virtuous desires grants
Mokshadam = liberation grants
Chaiva = and veritably
Omkaaraaya = the vibration of Om
Namo = salutations
Namaha = salutations supreme

Literal translation:

The Nada vibration of Om is the source of the primal singularity. Eternally meditated upon by the yogis, it grants all harmonious desires and the liberation of oneness with Unitive Consciousness. Salutations to the vibration of Om, the sacred Nada.

Poetic Translation:

OM, united with the source,
On which the Yogis ever dwell.
Grants desires and liberation,
Salutations to the Omkaaram.

Scientific Translation:

The Omkaaram Nada vibration is the primordial organizing principle of consciousness and the six dimensions of the Universe. It is experienced in the still minds of those who are aligned with the Unitive Field intention (c_i). It supports desires that resonate with Unitive Field intention (c_i), including the experience of oneness with Unitive Consciousness. Unending gratitude to the Nada vibration of Om.

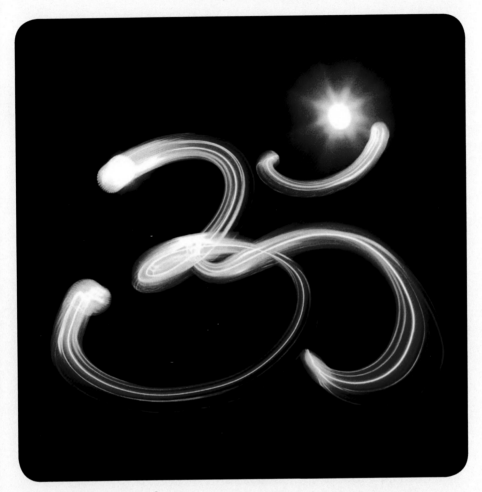

Om = E =mc^2. The ancient Sanskrit symbol for Om. The
Unitive Field's Hreem energy of causal intention (c_i) 10^{144}.

The entire universe is ultimately one living consciousness. The Unitive
Consciousness precisely creates a universe with stable environments so
that life forms with the hexagonal symmetry of carbon-based DNA life
can exist. The Unitive Consciousness guides the evolution of all life's
species directly and continually. The Unitive Consciousness continually
interacts with the DNA sequences and the protein activators of all living
organisms in accordance with the Law of Causation: $c_i{}^2 m = E$. This is
the driving force behind the evolution of species.

The intention of the Unitive Field is to nurture synergistic life forms in endless varieties that will ultimately evolve in consciousness to understand the functioning of the Unitive Field and to live in harmony with its nature. This is known as the state of yoga, oneness, or Unitive Consciousness.

What is called "dark energy" is actually the Nada Energy. It is the 10^{144} Hreem force of intention for the Unitive Field to nurture life in the universe. This sacred Nada vibration is also expressed in a six-verse intention. This is the causal intention of the Unitive Field toward its universe and life forms. This is the meaning of the sacred vibration of the Nada that is chanted eternally by the Unitive Field, to organize the universe and to nurture its beloved life forms:

Aloha I Ka Pono - An Aloha Anthem

I am, I sing for you,
I am, I give for you,
I live for you.
I am there for you.
I will care for you,
Forever and a day.

Ua Mau Ke Ea
O Ka ʻAina
I Ka Pono.
Forever is Sustained,
the Life of the Land,
by Righteousness.

We Pledge Our Harmony,
With One Ecology,
Living in Peace.
Synergy Prosperity, Sustainability,
Filled with Diversity,
Aloha for One and All!

The goal of the experience that we call life is to let this Nada energy fulfill its destiny of flowing through us. To accomplish this, we have to let go of our selfish desires and assume the Unitive Field causal intentions (c_i) for the universal wellbeing of creation. When we resonate with this Unitive intention, it can effortlessly flow through us; that is known as the state of Unitive Consciousness. In this state, our lives are easeful, peaceful, and useful.

The goal of life is to resonate with the Unitive Consciousness.

Chapter 4

What Is the Origin of the Universe's Primal Singularity, and What Caused the Big Bang?

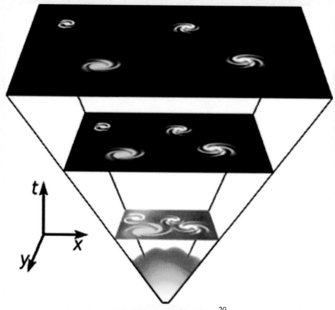

Big Bang Diagram[20]

I N THE STANDARD model of physics, there is no theory offered as to how the Universe began in the first place. Where did all of the consciousness, mass, and energy come from? What was there before the Big Bang? Where did the singularity come from? All of these important questions are left unanswered.

Unitive Field Theory offers compelling insight into these mysteries.

---

20 https://en.wikipedia.org/wiki/Big_Bang#/media/File:Universe_ expansion2.png

Variations of density within the Primordial Unitive Field of Nothingness.

Within the primordial Unitive Field of Nothingness were variations in the nothingness. No state, not even nothingness, is totally smooth or homogenous. In any field, areas of greater or lesser density will always exist. From these inherent differentiations of density by the Unitive Field Theory of The Electromagnetic Law of Attraction[21], The Unitive Field eventually divides itself into areas of lesser nothingness and denser nothingness, creating differentiation. The Unitive Field then assigns twelve values to these differentiations. It is able to create an attraction

---

21 The Unitive Field Theory of The Electromagnetic Law of Attraction will be
  described in more detail in Chapter 9.

between these twelve differentiations that generates a love energy field; that field becomes a spinning vortex, which generates the energy needed to create the singularity. The Unitive Field is able to transform this love energy into matter and to establish a controlled birth where the seed of the primal singularity expands to form the universe itself. The universe is comprised at its most basic level of Hreem energy—pure love energy that has the causal intention to know "Who am I?" and "How may I serve?" The universe is the altar upon which the Unitive Field worships and also expresses the twelve foundation values that it treasures. Once the universe is established, the Unitive Field nurtures its life forms continually.

At a certain point, without losing any of its energy or mass, it recycles the universe back into the primal singularity. The Unitive Field recalibrates with lessons learned and then rebirths the universe.

This is the eternal cycle of the Unitive Field. Life is the mirror that the Unitive Field creates to see itself and to share its joy.

The universe began as the seed of the primal singularity. The primordial energy within the singularity is generated by the Unitive Field Law of Causation:

$$c_i{}^2\,m = E$$

c_i = causal intention = intention to know "Who am I?"

and "How may I serve?"

m = the Unitive Field = the sum of all mass and energy

E = energy returned to the Unitive Field causal intention

Thus the Nada vibration is amplified into the energy contained in the primal singularity, which is pure consciousness. The primal singularity is the state in which the universe exists only in its first dimension of pure consciousness without space-time dimensions.

The primal singularity is a double tetrahedral pyramid generator.

The universe's most basic two-dimensional structure is a triangle, and the most basic three-dimensional structure is a tetrahedron.

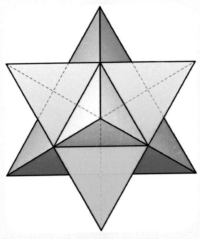

The Primal Singularity Double Tetrahedral structure from the perspective of the Z dimension

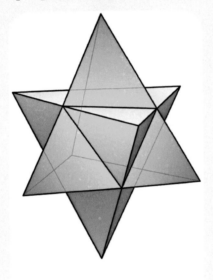

The Primal Singularity Double Tetrahedral structure from the perspective of the Y dimension

The singularity's Double Tetrahedral Pyramid Generator Composition

The singularity's downward pointing tetrahedral pyramid is comprised of the three intention pairs:

1. Gratitude – Simplicity

2. Cooperation – Love

3. Service – Unity

With an overall intention to understand: "Who am I?" the singularity's upward-pointing tetrahedral pyramid is comprised of three intention pairs:

1. Peace – Humility

2. Respect – Honesty

3. Happiness – Freedom

The overall intention is to make the universe work more effectively and efficiently. This intention is also expressed as "How may I serve?"

These six pairs of intentions correspond to the twelve types of elementary fermions: six quarks and six leptons.

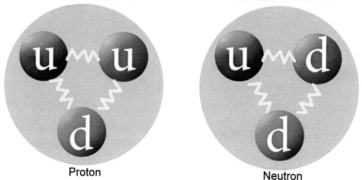

Proton   Neutron

Quark compositon of a proton and a netron (diagrams from *Wikipedia*)

The Quark positioning corresponds to the singularity's upward and downward pointing tetrahedral pyramids[22]

---

22 https://en.wikipedia.org/wiki/Quark

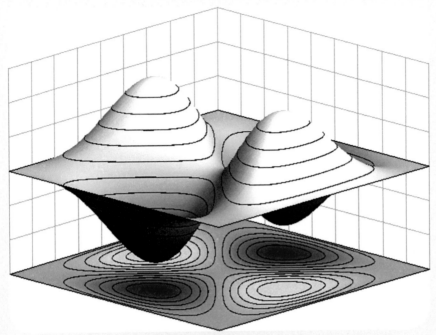

Antisymmetric wave function for a (fermionic) two-particle
state in an infinite square well potential. This diagram shows
that from a flat surface of nothing, areas of greater nothingness
and areas of lesser nothingness can be established. (Notice
the similarity of this wave function to the double tetrahedral
structure of the primal singularity.)[23]

The rotation of this double tetrahedral intention vortex is the motor
that powers the singularity and, eventually, the manifested universe.
The average duration of the dimension of time (t) from the universe's
reincarnation at the Big Birth (the Big Bang) to its return to the primal
singularity is approximately 144 billion years, which equates to one
billion years for each order of magnitude of the Unitive Field's causal
intention of (c_i) 10^{144} Hreem.

Within the primal singularity, the rotational energy gains momentum as
the Unitive Field of Consciousness increases the velocity of its rotation,
causing an increase in the Hreem and a corresponding increase in the
energy of the primal singularity.

23 Image - https://en.wikipedia.org/wiki/Fermion#/media/File:Asymmetricwave2.png

When the rotational energy within the primal singularity reaches the speed of light, it triggers the big birth, a precise quantity of the Hreem within the singularity forms Hreemium, the lightest and most plentiful subatomic element of the universe. Hreemium, in the standard model of particle physics, is referred to as "The Higgs boson," "The Higgs particle," or "The God particle." This elementary particle was confirmed on July 4, 2012 by experimentation done with The Large Hadron Collider.

The Unitive Field of Consciousness enjoys the bliss of its own attractive energy for each of its six intention pairs, which comprise the essential qualities of nature and the guidelines for natural selection.

1. Gratitude – Humility

2. Respect – Simplicity

3. Cooperation – Honesty

4. Happiness – Love

5. Service – Freedom

6. Peace – Unity

These qualities comprise the foundation of Unitive Consciousness.

During the primal singularity, the only dimension of the universe that exists is the first—Unitive Consciousness. The dimension of Time does not exist. Therefore, it is not possible to calculate how much time actually passes during the period of the primal singularity.

Space-time is created at the moment of the Big Bang. In Unitive Field Theory, this is referred to as the big birth, when the universe's dimension of Time (t) begins and the Hreem within the primal singularity transforms into the Universe's Hreem energy and most basic subatomic element, Hreemium, which together comprise what is known in the standard model of physics as:

1. Space

2. Time

3. Dark Energy

4. Dark Matter

5. Observable Energy

6. Observable Mass

The big birth is governed by the Unitive Field Law of Causation: $c_i^2 \, m = E$

The reason the Unitive Field manifests the additional five dimensions of the universe is that it is dedicated to knowing "Who am I?" by seeing its reflection in nature and in life forms. Its goal is to foster life forms that will ultimately appreciate, understand, and reflect the nature of the Unitive Field itself. It is a way that the Unitive Field can express love toward itself in another manifestation other than its own primal singularity Nada bliss experience.

The goal of the Unitive Field is to know itself by seeing its reflection in life forms.

The Relationship between the Universe's Primal Singularity Tetrahedron and the ancient Hebrew Tetragrammaton:

Truth is one and is expressed through various traditions in similar ways. The Omkaaram, the vibration of Om or the Nada, is represented by the vibration of Hreem. Hreem corresponds to the fourth energy center, the heart chakra, and vibrates at 432Hz (4x108). It is the vibration of DNA repair and the integration of the power of love into consciousness. Water or sand will form Cymatic Fibonacci spirals and sacred geometric patterns at this vibration. This vibration opens the heart to experiencing the loving energy of the Unitive Field.

The Hebrew Tetragrammaton displayed within a tetrahedron above the chapel altar at the Palace of Versailles in France[24]

---

24 https://en.wikipedia.org/wiki/Tetragrammaton#/media/File:Tetragra

The Tetragrammaton corresponds to the seventh energy center, the crown chakra, and has a vibration of 756 Hz (7x108). The Tetragrammaton is the same Nada energy flowing with the higher frequency of 756 Hz. It is the vibration of the return to spiritual order and wisdom. At this frequency, water or sand will form even more intricate Cymatic Fibonacci spirals and sacred geometric patterns. This vibration opens the crown chakra to the Unitive wisdom field.

According to Unitive Field Theory, the vowels for the Tetragrammaton are a fluctuation between Yiheev and Yiheevah. When a violin is played by a virtuoso violinist, the musician quivers the strings back and forth to create a fluctuation in the vibration of each note.

This vibrato adds a dimension of beauty and a depth of emotion to the music that is beyond that of a steady note. Similarly, the Tetragrammaton fluctuates between the vibration of Yiheev and Yiheevah. These are the vowels that give the optimal power to the Tetragrammaton; they are the ancient Hebrew vibrations for the sacred name of God, also known as Jahova, Yahova, or Yahweh. The Tetragrammaton's ancient Hebrew letters with vowels are as follows:

Yiheev is the vibration that corresponds to the universe's primal singularity's downward-pointing tetrahedral pyramid, which is comprised of the three intention pairs:

    1. Gratitude – Simplicity

    2. Cooperation – Love

    3. Service – Unity

The overall intention of these three pairs is to understand:"Who am I?"

Yiheevah is the vibration that corresponds to the primal singularity's upward-pointing tetrahedral pyramid, which is comprised of the three intention pairs:

1. Peace – Humility

2. Respect – Honesty

3. Happiness – Freedom

The overall intention of these three pairs is to make the universe work more effectively and efficiently. This intention is also expressed as "How may I serve?"

The vibrato of these vibrations creates the Tetragrammaton's sacred vibration, which aligns human consciousness with Unitive Consciousness.

The third of the Bible's Ten Commandments states, "Thou shalt not take the name of the Lord thy God in vain." Unitive Field Theory understands this command in the following way: The Tetragrammaton's vibrations are powerful and must be used for intentions in alignment with Unitive Field intention (c_i). According to Unitive Field Theory, the third commandment is understood to mean that the sacred names of the Unitive Field, such as the Tetragrammaton, should be meditated upon and recited for purposes in alignment with Unitive intention.

That means they should be incorporated into the consciousness of any being who aspires to attain Unitive Consciousness. They are one with the Nada energy and are vibrations for attuning the human mind with the Unitive mind. These sacred vibrations should be a living part of human consciousness and should not be feared or considered too sacred to recite. Their sanctity and purifying energy are for everyone who genuinely aspires to understand Unitive Consciousness. They are a powerful expression of the Nada energy. They are safe for all to use whose hearts are aligned with the intention of non-violence.

Truth Is One, Paths Are Many

In Unitive Field Theory, many sacred names of the Unitive Field are recognized as vibrations of the Nada. The Nada resonates with the vibrations of Aloha, Jahovah, Yahovah, Yiheeva, Allah, Keakua, and other sacred names of the Unitive Field. Unitive Field Theory recognizes the Nada vibration to be represented in all of the faiths included within the All Faiths Symbol in this book's dedication.

A core understanding of Unitive Field Theory is that each person ultimately has to be his or her own Guru. The world is here to offer us guidance on our path. Each person, by his or her own conscience, has to choose which path and wisdom are personally meaningful. Through each of the world's great spiritual paths, aspirants have attained Unitive Consciousness. Choose the path that resonates with your heart and follow it with all of your might for as long as it takes. If you are sincere in your aspirations by following your conscience and practicing the Golden Rule, your success is guaranteed. The force of the Unitive Field's causal intention of (c_i) 10^{144} Hreem is on your side. Ask and it shall be given; seek and you shall find. Your ultimate experience of oneness with Unitive Consciousness is assured.

The Spiritual Path.

Each person has to climb his or her own path to reach the ultimate goal. Others can guide us, but we have to choose our path and climb its steps to attain the ultimate state of Unitive Consciousness. Many paths lead to this ultimate state of oneness.

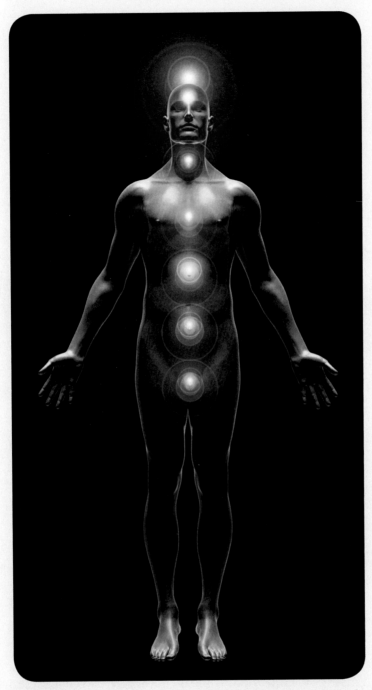

The six primary physic energy centers or chakras correspond to
the six dimensions of the universe.

Chapter 5

Will the Universe Continue to Expand, or Will It Contract Back into a Singularity?

IN ORDER TO enjoy the experience of life, one has to be fearless. The fear of death is the root of all fears. By understanding the immortality of the universe itself, we can understand our own immortality. All of nature moves in cycles; there are no one way trips. All of nature recycles the last body into the next bodies; there is no waste. Similarly, the universe as a whole is designed to be recyclable; what goes up will come down. The universal cycle starts with a primal singularity that births itself into a universe designed to foster a wide variety of life forms.

At the appropriate time, it reverses its outward expansion and begins to contract. Ultimately, the universe returns to the singularity without losing one atom, one joule of energy, or one bit of information.

The consciousness of the universe learns valuable lessons with each universal life cycle and births the new universe with even more precise laws to create even more stable environments for life to develop. The entire process is an expression of the love and service that the Unitive Field enjoys expressing as its body, the universe itself.

The universe is the Unitive Field expressing its love energy in six dimensions.

We are made of this same love energy, and if we allow ourselves to resonate with its vibration, it will animate our lives to express easefully the qualities of the Unitive Consciousness.

Nine Year Microwave Sky,[25] showing the infant universe's subtle mass-energy variations

According to Unitive Field Theory, there exists just one universe. It is not infinite in size. Its shape is similar to the shape of a galaxy.

Its lateral dimension (x) will expand to its full size of approximately 81 billion light years.

---

25 The detailed, all-sky picture of the infant universe created from nine years of WMAP data. The image reveals 13.77 billion year old temperature fluctuations (shown as color differences) that correspond to the seeds that grew to become the galaxies. The signal from our galaxy was subtracted using the multi-frequency data. This image shows a temperature range of ± 200 microKelvin.

Its longitudinal dimension (y) will expand to its full size of approximately 144 billion light years.

Its vertical dimension (z) will expand to approximately 21 billion light years.

Beyond these dimensions, the universe folds back into itself.

Therefore, by definition, there exists nothing that is outside of itself. Just as on a planet, if you go far enough in one direction, you will return to where you started; similarly, the universe is self-contained and there is no outside.

The universe will ultimately slow its expansion, begin to contract, and return to the primal singularity state.

According to Unitive Field Theory, this will happen when the sum total of the mass of all black holes equals approximately 38 percent of the total mass of the observable universe. This collective gravity will reverse the expansion of the universe and cause it to contract. The expansive era has a duration of approximately 72 billion years, and the contractive era is again approximately 72 billion years.

The cycle of the universe expanding—from the primal singularity and forming stars, solar systems, and galaxies, with abundant opportunities for life forms to develop, and then returning to the primal singularity—is an eternal cycle. It is the life cycle of the Unitive Field. The big birth (Big Bang) is the birth; the big reunion (big crunch) is the recycling back into the primal singularity.

The approximate time from big birth to big reunion is 144 billion years.

We are in this present universal life cycle at approximately 13.79 billion years since the big birth. Life forms in just 3 billion years within each universal life cycle, and it lasts until the big reunion. Within the primal singularity, the Unitive Consciousness recalibrates using the lessons learned from the last universal life cycle. It then births its next universe that is even more finely tuned than the last to create nurturing environments in which life can flourish.

From left to right: W. Nernst, A. Einstein, M. Planck, R.A. Millikan and von Laue at a dinner given by von Laue in Berlin on 11 November 1931[26]

Max Planck April 23, 1858 – October 4, 1947

Max Planck is considered to be the father of Quantum Physics. He was awarded the Nobel Prize in Physics in 1918 for his Quantum Theory. Plank integrated his understanding of science with his understanding of spirituality. Plank said in 1944, "As a man who has devoted his whole life to the most clear headed science, to the study of matter, I can tell you as a result of my research about atoms this much: There is no matter as such. All matter originates and exists only by virtue of a force which brings the particle of an atom to vibration and holds this most minute solar system of the atom together. We must assume behind this force the existence of a conscious and intelligent mind. This mind is the matrix of all matter."

Das Wesen der Materie [The Nature of Matter], speech at Florence, Italy (1944) (from Archiv zur Geschichte der Max-Planck-Gesellschaft, Abt. Va, Rep. 11 Planck, Nr. 1797)

---

26 https://en.wikipedia.org/wiki/Max_Planck#/media/File:Nernst,_Einstein,_
   Planck,_Millikan,_Laue_in_1931.jpg

Chapter 6

What Factors Cause the Speed of Light (c) to Change in Respect to the Universe's Dimension of Time (t)?

IT IS IMPORTANT to understand that the universe is one living organism that is eternal. It reincarnates at the end of each cycle. It is becoming more and more glorious with each birth. The diversity of life and its complexity will forever increase. To understand how the universe will return to the primal singularity and not just continue to expand forever, it is necessary to understand the change in the speed of light in relationship to the universe's dimension of time.

In astrophysics, the light signature of distant stars is analyzed through a science called spectroscopy. The spectrum characteristics of the light emitted from distant stars are examined, and if the light bands are shifted toward the red spectrum of light, it is inferred that this is caused by the source of the light moving away from the observer. If the light is shifted toward the blue end of the spectrum, it implies that the source is moving toward the observer. These shifts are caused by the Doppler effect on the light waves. The waves moving away will appear stretched and, therefore, these longer wavelengths are redder. The waves moving toward the observer will appear compressed and, therefore, these shorter wavelengths are bluer.

The current standard model of physics is misinterpreting the redshift observed in distant galaxies and assuming that the universe's speed of the expansion is increasing. This is not the case. The universe is expanding, but it is not increasing the speed of its expansion.

The added redshift that is being observed is an optical illusion, and the source of that optical illusion will be discussed in this chapter.

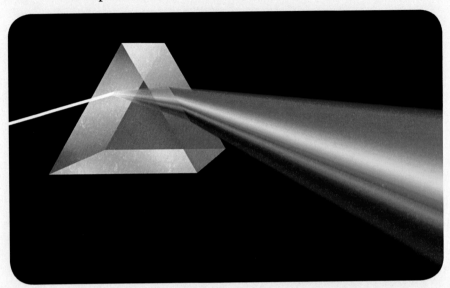

The Speed of Light is effected by the medium through which it is traveling.[27]

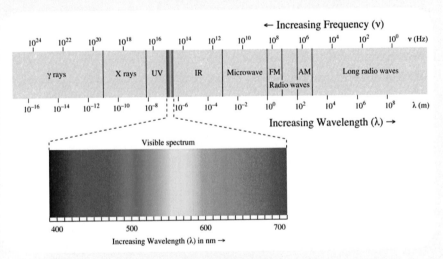

Visible light is only a narrow band within the Electromagnetic Wave Spectrum.[28]

---

27 You can view the image in motion at the site. https://en.wikipedia.org/wiki/Light
28 https://en.wikipedia.org/wiki/Light#/media/File:EM_spectrum.svg

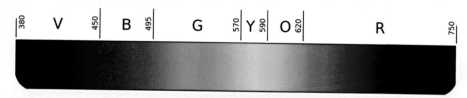

| 380 | V | 450 | B | 495 | G | 570 | Y | 590 | O | 620 | R | 750 |

Visible Light Spectrum[29]

In the current standard model of physics, it is assumed that the speed of light is a constant.

Therefore, it is postulated that the expansion of the universe is increasing in speed. This is based on the Doppler effect observed in the redshift of light seen from type 1A supernovae from distant galaxies. The more distant the galaxy, the greater the redshift observed. The assumption is that these distant galaxies are moving away from us at increasing speeds.

In Unitive Field Theory, the speed of light varies in relationship to time (t). The reason being that the density and temperature of the universe changes with time. Just after the big birth (the Big Bang), the universe was relatively small and dense and hot. As time (t) progresses, the universe spreads out and becomes less and less dense and cooler. As such, the medium through which light is passing becomes less and less dense.

This concept can be seen within our own solar system.

The photons leaving the sun's core take from 80,000 to 100,000 years to travel from where they are released by nuclear fusion in the core of the sun to the sun's surface. Even though they are traveling at their full light speed of 186,282 miles/second or 299,792,458 meters/second, they are bumping around through the dense medium of the sun. Then traveling at the same speed, through the less dense medium of space, it takes these same photons only 8 minutes and 20 seconds to travel the 93 million miles from the sun's surface to the earth. The reason for this difference is that even though the light is consistently traveling at the same speed, its actual progression in a given direction is determined by the density of the medium through which it travels.

---

29 https://en.wikipedia.org/wiki/Light#/media/File:Linear_visible_spectrum.svg

Therefore, the redshift that is thought to be the proof of the accelerating expansion of the universe is actually an optical illusion.

The light we are seeing today from distant galaxies was emitted from those galaxies over 13 billion years ago when the universe was much smaller and denser. Therefore, the actual progression of the light would have been slower. This is the reason why we observe their light to be redshifted; not because these galaxies are moving away from us at an accelerating speed.

If the standard model of physics were correct in this accelerated expansion theory, then all of space-time would be expanding. We would also have to observe this expansion within galaxies, but that is not the case. The earth is not increasing its distance from the sun.

Another factor in the optical illusion of this redshift appearance is the metallization of stars. Early stars had comparatively less heavy metals, which are formed in supernovae. Earlier stars were comprised of lighter elements, which gave a different light signature than the stars formed later in the universe evolution, which were formed of gases that had a greater percentage of heavy metals.

Still another factor in the optical illusion of redshift is that these early galaxies whose light is now reaching us from as little as 300,000 years after the big birth existed in a universe with fewer black holes. Therefore, the medium of space-time was much denser than the current later universe where matter has been thinned out by expansion and by the ever-growing appetite of super-massive black holes.

There is no observable force in the universe that can cause an increase in the speed of the universe's expansion.

According to Unitive Field Theory, only the expansive force of the big birth and the contractive gravitational force of the universe's collective mass-energy determine this expansion rate. Therefore, the universe's rate of expansion is not increasing. The universe will ultimately recycle back into the primal singularity, and not one atom, nor one joule of energy, nor one bit of information is lost in the process.

Unitive Field Theory predicts that the universe will reverse its expansion within 72 billion years from the big birth and will, within the next 72 billion years, contract and return to its primal singularity. This is an eternal cycle. What goes up will come down. All of nature moves in cycles; there are no one-way trips in nature. This universe will be recycled into the next universe.

What we call the speed of light is the speed of the progression of photons in a given direction. This speed changes in respect to the universe's density. The speed of the progression of photons in a given direction is speeding up as the universe expands and will again slow down as the universe contracts, and when it returns to the primal singularity, the speed of light will be zero and time will stop until the next big birth.

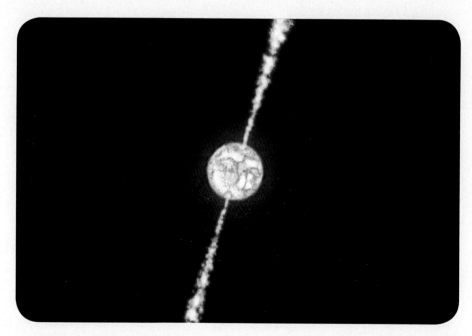

According to Unitive Field Theory, at the center of the universe is the Bindhu, a marble sized super dense core left behind from The Big Birth. It is the gravitational hub of the universe.

The observable universe merges back into the Bindhu every 144 billion years.

THE PROPHET

KAHLIL GIBRAN

GIBRAN'S MASTERPIECE
Illustrated with twelve full-page drawings by the author
Alfred·A·Knopf·Publisher·New·York

Kahlil Gibran; January 6, 1883 – April 10, 1931[30]

Kahlil Gibran's writings eloquently express the ecumenical wisdom of Unitive Field Theory. His mysticism is a convergence of several influences: Christianity, Islam, Sufism, Judaism and theosophy. He wrote: "You are my brother and I love you. I love you when you prostrate yourself in your mosque, and kneel in your church and pray in your synagogue. You and I are sons of one faith—the Spirit."[31]

His poetic expression of the Untitive Field intention of "How may I serve?" is expressed in his masterpiece *The Prophet*:

Then a ploughsman said, Speak to us of Work.

And he answered saying:

> You work that you many keep pace with
>
> The earth and the soul of the earth.
>
> For to be idle is to become a stranger
>
> unto the seasons, and to step out of life's
>
> procession, that marches in majesty and
>
> proud submission toward the infinite.
>
> …
>
> And in keeping yourself with labor
>
> you are in truth loving life,
>
> And to love life through labour is to be
>
> Intimate with life's inmost secret.
>
> …
>
> Work is love made visible.

---

30 http://www.newenglandhistoricalsociety.com/wp-content/uploads/2015/04/kahlil-gibran-The_Prophet_Cover.jpg

31 Alexandre Najjar, *Kahlil Gibran: A Biography*, Saqi, 2008, p.150

Chapter 7

What Are the Functions of Dark Matter, Dark Energy, and Black Holes?

I**T IS IMPORTANT** to understand that the universe is comprised of component parts that are like organs of its body, and each is necessary for the functioning of the whole.

There is not one wasted or unnecessary part. Every galaxy, star, planet, meteorite, or grain of dust is needed. Each life form is needed. You are a necessary part of the universe's functioning. Every part fits together with precision to allow the whole body of the universe to thrive. Nothing in the universe is unwanted or unneeded. Dark matter, dark energy, and black holes are essential components of the universe. Their functions are the focus of this chapter.

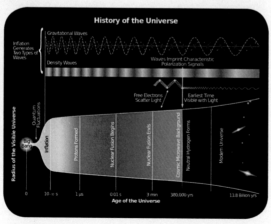

History of the Universe - gravitational waves are hypothesized to arise from cosmic inflation, an expansion just after the Big Bang.[32]

---

32 https://en.wikipedia.org/wiki/Big_Bang#/media/File:History_of_the_Universe.svg

The Formation of Hreemium

At each big birth (Big Bang), a precise quantity of the Hreem energy in the singularity converts into the universe's most basic particle, Hreemium. This Hreemium manifests itself as the universe, and it is comprised of the following components:

Visible Mass and Energy

This 4.9 percent of the universe comprises all of the energy and mass that can be observed. This includes all galaxies and clusters. This is the universe that we can observe. The other approximately 95 percent of the universe is the framework that holds it together and animates it.

This 5 percent ratio is similar to the ratio of the size of any planet to the size of that planet's biosphere. The biosphere, where life actually lives on planet Earth, is approximately 5 percent of the mass of planet Earth, and it forms the most delicate and diverse ecosystems.

The 95 percent balance of the universe has as its function the sustainment of this 5 percent. Within these protected biosphere domes, the flower of life blooms and flourishes, and the raison d'etre of the universe is fulfilled.

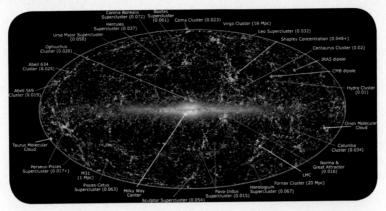

The visible universe's mass-energy—of solar systems forming galaxies rotating around black holes—comprises approximately [33] 4.9 percent of the universe's total mass.

---

33 https://en.wikipedia.org/wiki/Big_Bang#/media/File:2MASS_LSS_char t-NEW_
   Nasa.jpg

Dark Matter

Dark matter is invisible. Based on the effect of gravitational lensing, a ring of dark matter has been inferred in this image of a galaxy cluster (CL0024+17) and has been represented in blue.[34]

Dark matter is Hreemium that is on all scales evenly distributed and is present in all space-time. It comprises approximately 26.8 percent of the universe's mass and forms the framework that stabilizes the universe, similar to the bones of a body. Dark matter does not move or change. Although it does vibrate with the Nada, its distribution state is homogenous and is not withdrawn back into the primal singularity during the universe's life cycles. As such, it cannot be detected with scientific instruments because it is evenly distributed everywhere. Scientific instruments are only capable of measuring changes in matter or energy.

34 https://en.wikipedia.org/wiki/Dark_matter#/media/File:CL0024%2B17.jpg

The Unitive Field of Hreemium is not changing and, therefore, cannot be detected. However, it can be understood as essential for how light is able to travel. Empty space is not a vacuum; it is filled with Hreemium or dark matter. That is why light, which is an electromagnetic wave, is able to travel. All electromagnetic waves need a medium through which to travel. Hreemium is the medium through which light travels and forms the Unitive Field that supports the universe.

Dark Energy

The balance of the Hreem energy of the singularity that did not convert into Hreemium expresses itself as the so-called "dark energy." It comprises the energy needed for the Unitive Field to animate the universe and is approximately 68.3 percent of the universe's mass.

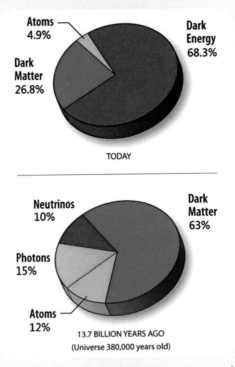

Estimated distribution of matter and energy in the universe, today (top) and when the CMB was released (bottom)[35]

---

35 https://en.wikipedia.org/wiki/Dark_matter#/media/File:080998_Universe_
Content_240_after_Planck.jpg

Black Holes

Black Hole[36]

In order for life to be fostered, great stability in planetary systems is needed for millions of years. To provide this security in galaxies, a strong hub is needed. Super-massive black holes are located in the center of all galaxies to provide the gravitation attraction needed for their orbiting stars to have a steady orbit. Black holes are also the clocks that regulate the lifespan of each universal cycle, and at the right time, they trigger the big reunion.

Summary of Dark Matter, Dark Energy, and Black Holes' Functions

There is nothing negative or violent in the universe. Every part of the universe is harmonious and serves to fulfill the causal intentions of the Unitive Field. Dark energy, dark matter, and black holes are all positive energies and formations essential to the universe's preservation and stability. They are essential for the universe's ability to foster life.

---

36 https://en.wikipedia.org/wiki/Black_hole#/media/File:BH_LMC.png

The Big Reunion

According to Unitive Field Theory, there exists a super-dense core of the universe that remains after the Big Birth. This is called The Bindhu. It is the gravitational hub of the universe as well as the sacred source and abode of the Nada vibration and the Unitive Consciousness that is the source of the universe.

The observable universe returns to the Bindhu every 144 billion years. This return is known as the Big Reunion. The Big Reunion is triggered when approximately 21 percent of the mass of the observable universe is contained within its black holes.

Recalibration within the Primal Singularity

At each big reunion, the observable universe returns to the primal singularity. In this state, the universe exists only in its first dimension of consciousness. The approximate 4.9 percent mass and energy that comprises the observable universe is returned into Hreemium; then it is returned into pure Hreem energy within the primal singularity where the Unitive Consciousness digests the last universal cycle's experiences and recalibrates for the next big birth.

The standard model of physics postulates that the size of the primal singularity is smaller than an atom. According to Unitive Field Theory, the size of the primal singularity is much larger—closer to the size of a marble (1.3 to 2.54 cm) in diameter. Within this primal singularity is compressed the total mass-energy of the observable Universe. This is not as incomprehensible as it might appear. What we call matter is comprised of 99.9999999…percent empty space. And all the positive energy charges of the universe equal all of its negative energy charges, so the flow of energy is just an attempt to balance out energy fluctuations that ultimately cancel each other out. So it is understandable that the Universe is able to expand from a marble-sized, super-dense primal singularity into an expanded universe and then again retract back into its seed form. This is the eternal cycle of the Unitive Consciousness.

Return of the universe to the primal singularity from the perspective of the Y Dimension.

Return of the universe to the primal singularity from the perspective of the Z Dimension.

Sri Swami Sivananda
September 8, 1887 - July 14, 1963[37]

Sri Swami Sivananda was one of the greatest yoga masters of the 20th century. He was a Physician, Monk, founder of The Divine Life Society, and Sivananda Ashram on the banks of the Ganges in Rishikesh, India in 1936. He is the author of over 200 books on Yoga, Health, and Vedanta. In 1945, he organized the All-World Religions Federation. Swami Sivananda merged the various branches of Yoga into one holistic approach that he called "The Yoga of Synthesis." Through his students, Yoga has spread throughout the world.

His summary teachings were carved on the Ashram's Sivananda Pillar and are sung as a devotional kirtan.

"Serve, Love, Give, Purify, Meditate, Realize,

Do Good, Be Good, Be Kind, Be Compassionate."

This is the essence of Unitive Field Theory.

---

37 The Divine Life Society: www.dlshq.org

Chapter 8

What Is the One Force that Unites the Four Forces in the Standard Model of Physics—the Strong Force, the Weak Force, Gravity, and Electromagnetism?

U LTIMATELY, THE UNIVERSE is one consciousness. All of its laws manifest from one principle of nature. Consciousness, expressing itself as electromagnetism, is the one force unifying the four forces of nature.

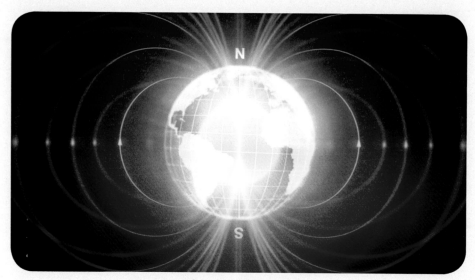

Electromagnetism

The standard model of physics assumes that four independent forces govern matter and energy.

Those forces are:

1. **The strong force**: governing the nuclear bonds of atoms.

2. **The weak force**: governing atomic radioactive decay.

3. **Electromagnetism**: governing the alignment and flow of charged particles and their corresponding magnetic fields.

4. **Gravity**: The force of attraction between all mass-energy.

According to Unitive Field Theory, the one primary force that is the basis of these four forces of nature is electromagnetism.

The weak force, the strong force, and gravity are all different manifestations of electromagnetism.

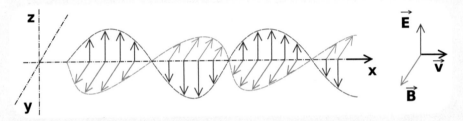

All Electromagnetic energy flows in waves at the speed of light.
They comprise the brainwaves of the one consciousness
that pervades the universe.[38]

The standard model of physics believes that in all situations concerning magnetism, opposite charges attract and like charges repel.

In Unitive Field Theory, it is proposed that, with sufficient pressure and temperature, these magnetic properties can be reversed so that like charges will attract. The term within Unitive Field Theory for this state is "electromagnetic resonance." During the state of electromagnetic resonance, like charges resonate with like charges. Electromagnetic resonance occurs under extreme pressures that compress the energy of the electrons from their normal rotational shells into the nuclei of their atoms.

---

38 Image source: https://en.wikipedia.org/wiki/Electromagnetic_radiation#/media/
   File:Onde_electromagnetique.svg

The great pressure and temperature needed to produce electromagnetic resonance occur in only four places in nature:

1. **A Supernova**: Super-massive stars can maintain their nuclear fusion reactions for all of their elements, which are lighter in atomic weight than iron. When these stars begin to fuse their iron, it marks the end of the star's current incarnation, for iron cannot fuse into heavier elements within a star. Therefore, the star's expansive nuclear force cannot be sustained. The star's contractive force of gravity then prevails, and within seconds, the star collapses in what is called a supernova. The force of the imploding star has enough heat and pressure to force the electrons within its atoms into the nuclei of their atoms, thereby creating electromagnetic resonance. When this happens, heavier elements are fused, which provides the explosive nuclear energy that powers the supernova.

A type Ia supernova (bright spot on the bottom-left) near a galaxy[39]

39 https://en.wikipedia.org/wiki/Supernova#/media/File:SN1994D.jpg

2. **Super-Massive Black Holes**: When mass is sucked into super-massive black holes, the pressure and heat are sufficient to create electromagnetic resonance, which fuses these elements into heavier elements and releases its nuclear energy in the form of quasars.

An artist's concept of a black hole with a corona[40]

3. **Neutron stars** are formed when massive stars that have an initial mass of at least 8 times the mass as our sun collapse in a supernova. The extreme pressure and heat of the implosion causes electromagnetic resonance as the electrons of the atoms are forced into their nuclei, thereby forming neutrons.

Electromagnetic resonance allows matter to become so dense that one tablespoon of a neutron star has an equivalent mass of over 2700 Great Pyramids of Giza. Some neutron stars have twice the mass of our sun yet are only 22 kilometers (14 miles) in diameter. They can rotate at 43,000 revolutions per minute and emit strong electromagnetic radiation from their poles known as pulsars.

---

40 https://en.wikipedia.org/wiki/Black_hole#/media/File:Black_Holes_Monsters_in_
Space.jpg

Radiation from the pulsar PSR B1509-58, a rapidly spinning neutron star, makes nearby gas glow in the X-ray spectrum as seen in gold detected by the Chandra X-ray Space Telescope. The blue and the red depict infrared radiation that is detected by the Wise infrared space telescope and illuminates the rest of the nebula, from the WISE infrared wavelength space telescope.[41]

4. **Within the Universe's Primal Singularity**: Within the primal singularity, the entire mass of the observable universe is compressed into a space the size of a marble. This is done through electromagnetic resonance. The big birth (Big Bang) is powered by the release of this resonance, so that like charges now repel each other; this repulsive force powers the universe's expansion. This force changes Hreem energy into Hreemium and starts the clock ticking for the universe's next incarnation.

41 https://en.wikipedia.org/wiki/Neutron_star#/media/File:PIA18848-PSRB1509-58-ChandraXRay-WiseIR-20141023.jpg

Within the marble-sized Primal Singularity is contained all
of the Mass-Energy of the Universe. This compacted state is
possible because of Electromagnetic Resonance.

The Weak Force is a Manifestation of Electromagnetism

The weak force, or weak interaction, is responsible for the radioactive decay of subatomic particles, and plays an essential role in nuclear fission as first described by Lise Meitner in 1938. Enrico Fermi proposed the first theory of weak interaction, known as Fermi's interaction in 1933.

The Standard Model of particle physics describes electromagnetism and the weak force as two different aspects of a single electroweak interaction, the theory of which was developed around 1968 by Sheldon Glashow, Abdus Salam, and Steven Weinberg. They were awarded the 1979 Nobel Prize in Physics for their work.[42]

In Unitive Field Theory, it is proposed that the weak force is simply the release of electromagnetic resonance into common electromagnetism.

42 https://en.wikipedia.org/wiki/Weak_interaction

Albert Einstein envisioned Gravity as a Curvature of Spacetime.

The Force of Gravity is Electromagnetic

Both the force and gravity and the force of electromagnetism share one revealing similarity. The force of attraction between any two masses for both gravity and electromagnetism is inversely proportional to the square of the distance between them. That means if the distance between the masses is twice as far, the attraction will be one quarter the strength.

According to Unitive Field Theory, gravity is actually a manifestation of electromagnetism.

It is a proven scientific fact that the attractive force of magnetism is in all domains of nature stronger than its repulsive force. In Unitive Field Theory, this fact is known as the Electromagnetic Law of Attraction. (We'll discuss the Electromagnetic Law of Attraction more thoroughly in the next chapter.) The universe itself favors attraction over repulsion.

As such, the force in the standard model called gravity is that subtle weak differentiation between the electromagnetic force of attraction and the electromagnetic force of repulsion in all mass-energy in the universe. Gravity is the sum total of all electromagnetic attractions, less all electromagnetic repulsions.

The Strong Force is the Force of Electromagnetic Resonance

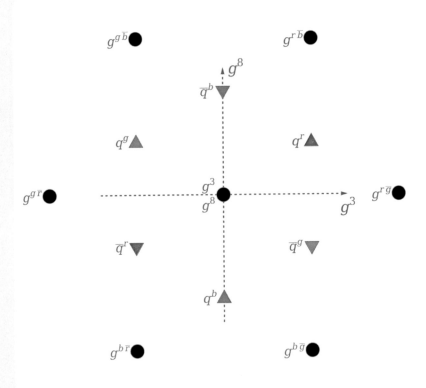

The pattern of strong charges for the three colors of quark, three antiquarks, and eight gluons (with two of zero charge overlapping).[43]

Reference: The drawing above is of the strong force's alignment of quarks and gluons.

---

43 https://commons.wikimedia.org/wiki/File:QCD.svg

Below is the same diagram as above, but now with the dots connected.

This displays the actual force lines of The Strong Force that binds together the nuclei of atoms. Note that the strong force is arranged in a double tetrahedral force field, generating a hexagonal force field.

The Strong Force fields that bind together the nuclei of atoms

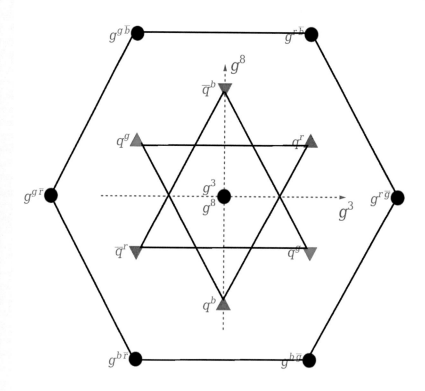

This same pattern exists in the primal singularity with the six pairs of foundational values that are the source of the Hreem energy that powers the universe. This same pattern exists in all dimensions of the universe and is the substructure of the Unitive Field.

In summary, according to Unitive Field Theory, the four forces of nature are manifestations of just one force, Consciousness, expressing itself as electromagnetism.

Sri Swami Satchidananda
December 22, 1914 - August 19, 2002

Sri Swami Satchidananda was one of the most widely respected Yoga Masters of our time. He was a world leader in promoting interfaith harmony. He was the founder of Integral Yoga International, which serves in sharing the ancient wisdom of Yoga and plant-based nutrition on every continent. His life and teachings express the essence of Unitive Field Theory.

"The dedicated ever enjoy supreme peace. Therefore, live only to serve."[44]
— Sri Swami Satchidananda

---

44 www.SwamiSatchidananda.Org

Chapter 9

What Is the Force that Generates the Rotational Spin of All Matter from the Microcosm of the Atom to the Macrocosm of a Galaxy?

IT IS IMPORTANT for the consciousness of humanity to align with Unitive Consciousness. This alignment is the ultimate goal of the experience that we call life. Unitive Consciousness manifests as nature, and its attributes can be understood by examining nature. In electromagnetism, the unifying force of nature—the Electromagnetic Law of Attraction— is demonstrated. In all realms of nature, the power of attraction is more powerful than the power of repulsion. The scientific proof for "The Electromagnetic Law of Attraction" is given in this chapter. This law governs not only matter but also the evolution of life forms. Life forms that are symbiotic with other organisms, that enhance biodiversity and enrich their environments, will thrive and become branches on the tree of life. Those organisms that are parasitic to other species and deplete nature will not long endure. This is the true force animating natural selection. Nature favors attraction over repulsion.

This same truth stands for civil organization, corporations, and governments. Ruling by coercion, fear, or other types of repulsive forces is not as strong as ruling with cooperation, love, or other types of attractive forces. Nature always favors attractive forces for they are aligned with loving service, which is the strongest force in the Unitive Field.

The visible light spectrum displays the same star tetrahedral matrix that is found throughout nature.

The Unitive Field Theory of Asymmetry

The Theory of Asymmetry is also known as the Theory of Dynamic Motion. According to this theory, in all dimensions of the universe, a certain amount of randomness or unevenness exists to ensure that a perfect equilibrium or state of static stability is never possible.

The reason for this primary theory is that if perfect balance were ever to exist at any point in time, the universe would have no reason to move from that point, so it would, therefore, remain still or static. To prevent this stagnant state and to insure that the universe's primary intention, to know "Who am I?" and "How may I serve?" is advanced, the universe is inherently in dynamic movement. All mass and all energy must continually rotate and revolve, and the universe as a whole must either expand or contract.

The Unitive Field Theory of The Electromagnetic Law of Attraction

Unitive Field Theory postulates that the primary force that generates the universe's Asymmetry is the imbalance between the force of attraction and the force of repulsion in electromagnetism. This force in Unitive Field Theory is referred to as "The Electromagnetic Law of Attraction." Every atom and all mass in the universe generate electromagnetic fields. These electromagnetic fields are comprised of a collection of individual field lines that radiate from the north pole to the south pole of the atom, planet, star, black hole, or galaxy. These invisible field lines can be seen in the alignment of iron filings in the presence of a magnet. Each of these field lines itself has one side that has an attractive force and one side that has a repulsive force. The electromagnetic attractive force is slightly stronger than the electromagnetic repulsive force, and this electromagnetic differentiation is the primary force for the universe's asymmetry.

The implication of this imbalance is that the stronger force of attraction generates a spin on the axis of all matter from an atom to a planet to a star to a galaxy. Just as an electric motor spins because of the force of electromagnetic attraction, so all of nature's bodies, from the microcosm of atoms to the macrocosm of galaxies are spinning with this same force. Atoms are miniature electric motors, and galaxies spin with the torque of their combined mass-energy.

Spiral Galaxies exhibit Fibonacci spiral patterns

This theory also explains why the mass at the center of all galaxies is rotating and revolving at speeds that are greater than the speed of mass farther out in their galaxies. The combined mass of their central super-massive black holes and the stars within the central areas of galaxies have a relatively great combined mass and, therefore, an electromagnetic field so powerful that its force of The Electromagnetic Law of Attraction causes the galaxies' central areas to spin very quickly.

This differentiation in the force of the attractive and repulsive force of electromagnetism also explains the amazing speeds of the rotations of neutron stars, which are the super-dense remains of supernovae.

They are the densest matter in the universe other than the singularities of black holes. Neutron stars can have twice the mass of our sun, yet they are only 22 kilometers (14 miles) in diameter. The Electromagnetic Law of Attraction is the force that can cause them to rotate at over 1,000 revolutions per second!

The Electromagnetic Law of Attraction is the primary force propelling the singularity of a black hole to rotate at speeds up to 81 percent of the speed of light.

The Electromagnetic Law of Attraction is the main reason why a star's corona is a higher temperature than a star's surface. Electromagnetic differentiation causes the electromagnetic bands emitted from the star's surface to twist and, thereby, short-circuit, thus forming lightning-like sparks that generate the star's energetic explosions called coronal mass ejections.

A comparable electromagnetic force that exists on earth is lightning. Lightning is also hotter than the sun's surface. The sun's electromagnetic bands are like huge bands of lightning that project from the sun and can grow to be thousands of miles in diameter. When they twist and short-circuit with each other, the released electromagnetic energy creates temperatures that are magnitudes higher than the sun's surface. The twisting of these bands, projecting from the sun's surface, is caused by the Electromagnetic Law of Attraction. The bands twist because their field's attractive forces are stronger than their repulsive forces.

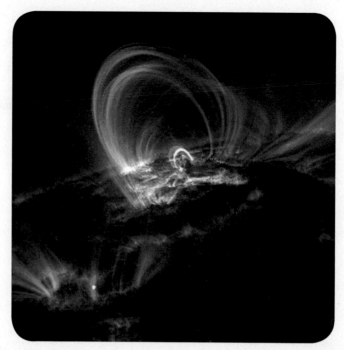

Coronal Electromagnetic Loops[45]

Electromagnetic force is the reason why the quasars emitted from black holes exit the black hole along the lines of its axis. Supernovae also explode with the majority of the force projected along the lines of its axis. The axis is perpendicular to the celestial body's rotation, which means that the axis projects from the celestial body's magnetic poles. Matter and energy will predominantly follow this line when mass or energy is ejected from a celestial body, including a singularity. It is the reason for the elliptical shape of galaxies and of the universe itself.

Because of centrifugal force, all galaxies, as well as the universe as a whole, are relatively flattened.

The rotation caused by electromagnetic differentiation is the force that manifests the patterns of Fibonacci spiral sequences, which are seen in nature on every scale and will be described in more detail in the next chapter.

---

45 https://commons.wikimedia.org/wiki/File:Traceimage.jpg

The direction of the spin can be calculated with the same right hand rule used for determining the direction of electromagnetic field lines.

The combined electromagnetic force of a galaxy is the primary force that determines its direction and speed of rotation. When two galaxies collide and merge, their new combined electromagnetic force determines the new merged galaxy's rotational direction and velocity.

Diagrams showing the cause of the Unitive Field

Electromagnetic Law of Attraction

The attraction between magnets is a little stronger than the repulsion. That is due to the alignment of the molecular magnets in the magnet.

The attraction as well as the repulsion of magnets decreases significantly with increasing distance.

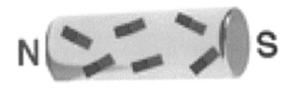

Normal alignment of the molecular magnets[46]

When two equal magnets touch each other, the attraction between two unequal poles is 5-10 percent stronger than the repulsion of equal poles. That is due to the alignment of the molecular magnets in a magnet. In a single magnet, the molecular magnets are aligned sort of parallel to each other. The more regular the molecular magnets are aligned, the higher the magnet's "strength."

---

46 All three magnet images are courtesy of Supermagnete:
   http://www.supermagnete.de/eng/faq/Is-the-attraction-between-magnets-as- high-as-
   the-repulsion?big=236%23pu236

Attraction

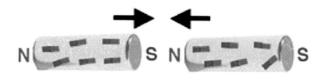

Improved alignment of the molecular magnets during attraction

When two unequal magnetic poles attract each other, the one magnet supports the parallel alignment of the molecular magnets in the other magnet. This renders both magnets a little stronger.

Repulsion

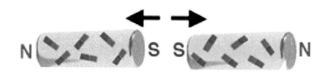

Reduced alignment of the molecular magnets during repulsion

When two equal magnetic poles repel each other, the one magnet disturbs the parallel alignment of the molecular magnets in the other magnet. This renders both magnets a little weaker. If you pull them far enough apart, however, they regain their original order and, therefore, their original strength.

In summary, The Unitive Field Electromagnetic Law of Attraction shows that the difference in the force of attraction and the force of repulsion in electromagnetism is the driving force that animates the spins and rotations that are present in the universe from atoms to galaxy clusters.

The Light of Truth Universal Shrine (LOTUS), in Virginia, is a unique temple dedicated to the Interfaith ideal that "Truth is One, Paths are Many."[47]

The central light column symbolizes the Light of Truth that illuminates all faiths.

The light column rises and divides to illuminate each of the altars. This vision of Swami Satchidananda was designed, engineered, and installed by Fredrick Swaroop Honig and Dr. Paul Prasant Hansma.

47 www.LOTUS.org

Chapter 10

What Are the Forces that Cause the Universe's Recurring Hexagonal Patterns and Logarithmic Fibonacci Spiral Sequences?

THE FORCES OF electromagnetic differentiation, combined with the gravitational and centrifugal forces, form the classic signature of the Unitive Field's manifestation, the logarithmic spirals that are predominant in every magnitude of nature. These spirals, known in Unitive Field Theory as the Nadaroopa, are the fingerprint of the Unitive Field and are present in all six of the Universe's dimensions.

Correlation between Seed and Plant

Just as a seed breeds a plant that has similar qualities to the seed itself, so the singularity manifests as a universe with similar qualities to itself.

The singularity vortex is a double tetrahedral pyramid with hexagonal symmetry. Therefore, hexagonal symmetry is the organizing principle of the universe and life itself, from a snowflake to the carbon atom that is the basis of DNA and life.

Fibonacci Sequences and Spiral Patterns

Leonardo Fibonacci (c. 1170 – c. 1250) brought the long-established mathematical wisdom of India to Europe

Leonardo Fibonacci (c. 1170 – c. 1250) was an Italian mathematician, considered to be "the most talented Western mathematician of the Middle Ages."[48]

---

48 https://en.wikipedia.org/wiki/Fibonacci.

Other sources for this discussion of Fibonacci include: Singh, Pamanand (1985). "The so-called fibonacci numbers in ancient and medieval India." *Historia Mathematica* 12: 229–244.

Goonatilake, Susantha (1998). *Toward a Global Science.* Indiana University Press. p. 126.

Knuth, Donald (2006). *The Art of Computer Programming: Generating All Trees – History of Combinatorial Generation.* Volume 4. Addison-Wesley. p. 50.

Hall, Rachel W. "Math for Poets and Drummers." *Math Horizons* 15 (2008) p. 10–11.

Fibonacci Numbers from The On-Line Encyclopedia of Integer Sequences.

Fibonacci popularized the Hindu-Arabic numeral system in the Western World, primarily through his composition in 1202 of *Liber Abaci* (Book of Calculation). He also introduced to Europe the sequence of Fibonacci numbers, which he used as an example in *Liber Abaci*. In that work, he also introduced and advocated using the so-called modus Indorum (method of the Indians), today known as Arabic numerals. He first proposed numeration with the digits 0–9 and place value. The book showed the practical importance of the new numeral system by applying it to commercial bookkeeping, conversion of weights and measures, the calculation of interest, money-changing, and other applications. The book was well-received throughout educated Europe and had a profound impact on European thought.

The Ancient Numeral System of India became known as The Hindu-Arabic Numeral System:

੦	੧	੨	੩	੪	੫	੬	੭	੮	੯
0	1	2	3	4	5	6	7	8	9

The significance of the development of the positional number system is probably best described by the French mathematician Pierre Simon Laplace (1749–1827) who wrote:

> It is India that gave us the ingenious method of expressing all numbers by the means of ten symbols, each symbol receiving a value of position, as well as an absolute value; a profound and important idea which appears so simple to us now that we ignore its true merit, but its very simplicity, the great ease which it has lent to all computations, puts our arithmetic in the first rank of useful inventions, and we shall appreciate the grandeur of this achievement when we remember that it escaped the genius of Archimedes and Apollonius, two of the greatest minds produced by antiquity.

Although Fibonacci's *Liber Abaci* contains the earliest known description of the sequence outside of India, the sequence had been noted by Indian mathematicians as early as the sixth century.

In the Fibonacci sequence of numbers, each number is the sum of the previous two numbers. Fibonacci began the sequence 0, 1, 1, 2, 3, 5, 8, 13, 21, 34, 55, 89, 144, 233, 377.

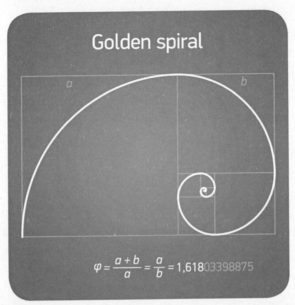

Golden spiral

$$\varphi = \frac{a+b}{a} = \frac{a}{b} = 1{,}61803398875$$

Phi is the basis for the Golden Ratio, Section or Mean. The ratio, or proportion, determined by Phi (1.618 …) was known to the Greeks as "dividing a line in the extreme and mean ratio" and to Renaissance artists as the "Divine Proportion." It is also called the Golden Section, Golden Ratio, and the Golden Mean.

The Golden Ratio is seen in sea shells such as the Nautilus shell.

The Golden Ratio is seen in the arrangement of leaves on a plant. In botany, phyllotaxis or phyllotaxy is the arrangement of leaves on a plant stem (from Ancient Greek phýllon "leaf " and "táxis" arrangement). Phyllotactic spirals form a distinctive class of patterns in nature.[49]

Cyclones develop with the Golden Ratio. Here are three tropical cyclones of the Pacific typhoon season at different stages of development. The weakest (left) demonstrates only the most basic circular shape. A stronger storm (top right) demonstrates spiral banding and increased centralization, while the strongest (lower right) has developed an eye.[50]

---

49 https://en.wikipedia.org/wiki/Phyllotaxis#/media/File:Aloe_polyphylla_1.jpg
50 https://en.wikipedia.org/wiki/Tropical_cyclone#/media/File:Typhoon_ saomai_060807.jpg

Spiral Galaxies also are organized in alignment with The Golden Ratio. An example of a spiral galaxy, the Pinwheel Galaxy (also known as Messier 101 or NGC 5457)[51]

Fibonacci sequences appear throughout nature from the arrangements of the seeds on a sunflower to the spiral arms of galaxies. This is because within the seed of the singularity, the Hreem Unitive Consciousness itself is arranged in Fibonacci sequences. The glory of Unitive Consciousness is one with this fingerprint. This is the pattern of the Nada itself.

The sacred Nada vibration causes the Unitive Field to align and arrange itself into this pattern in all space, time, and dimensions. This is the expression of Nada energy in matter. The universe, ultimately, is this one repeating pattern expressed in unique ways. This pattern in Unitive Field Theory is known as the Nadaroopa.

51 http://www.spacetelescope.org/news/html/heic0602.html (direct link)

The Nadaroopa — God's Fingerprint

The Nadaroopa is the golden ratio Fibonacci sequence pattern that repeats throughout nature

The Nadaroopa is the form that the Nada vibration creates in consciousness and in matter. From the arrangement of the Hreem consciousness within the singularity to the manifested universe, the Unitive Field fingerprint is a mandala (shown above) permeating all dimensions of the Unitive Field.

The Nadaroopa is the organizing force for the Fibonacci spirals pervading the universe. It can be seen throughout nature. Below it is seen in the layout of the seeds of a sunflower.

The Nadaroopa
Sunflower seed pattern

The Nadaroopa, the
fingerprint of God

The Unitive Field Theory: Consciousness is the seed of matter.

Unitive Field Theory shows that consciousness is the seed of matter and that matter does not create consciousness. This theory is consistent with sacred geometry and the hexagonal patterns and Fibonacci sequences that permeate the universe and its life forms on all scales.

Unitive Field Theory: Life is based on hexagonal symmetry.

The building block upon which DNA is structured is the carbon atom with atomic number 6. It forms a variety of hexagonal structures from DNA to diamonds. It has the strongest bonds known to nature since they are aligned with the same six-pointed symmetry found in the strong force, in Hreemium, and in the six pairs of principal values.

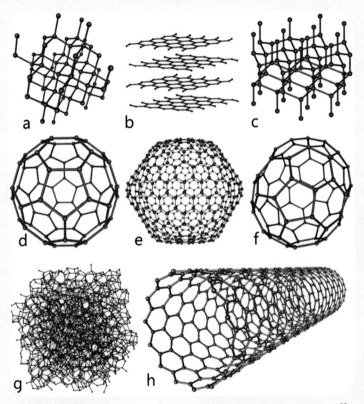

"Eight Allotropes of Carbon," created by Michael Ströck[52]

52 Licensed under CC BY-SA 3.0 via Wikimedia Commons: https://commons. wikimedia.org/wiki/File:Eight_Allotropes_of_Carbon.png

The Nada vibration is composed of six pairs of values that generate a universe with six dimensions expressing hexagonal symmetry. All life forms are organized with hexagonal symmetry. DNA is carbon-based, with the hexagonal symmetry of an atom with six protons, six neutrons, and six electrons. Water is the basis of life and crystallizes in the six-pointed symmetrical structures comprising all ice crystals. These hexagonal crystals express the vibrational qualities present in water atoms when they freeze. Life itself is the eloquent expression of the hexagonal nature of creation. These six dimensions define the universe's hexagonal organizing principles, which are repeated throughout nature.

Water is the mother of life and, like carbon-based DNA, exhibits hexagonal symmetry. Water has been shown to have memory and consciousness.[53]

53 "Water, Consciousness & Intent" Dr. Masaru Emoto: https://www.youtube.com/ watch?v=vdGhDXTQB7c Water's Memories ~ The Mystery of Water ~ Scientific Proof:

Note that snowflakes are each unique yet are all have hexagonal symmetry.

Chapter 11

What Is the Source of Life in the Universe and What Governs Its Evolution?

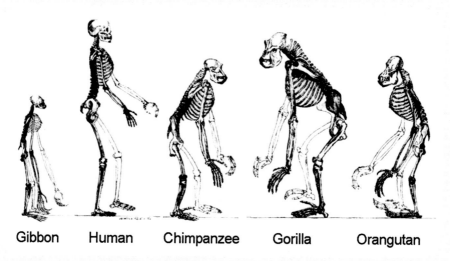

| Gibbon | Human | Chimpanzee | Gorilla | Orangutan |

All hominoids are descendants of a common ancestor.[54]

ACCORDING TO UNITIVE Field Theory, all life forms in the universe derive from just one genesis and share in common at least 6 percent of their DNA. The Unitive Field's causal intention (ci) 10^{144} Hreem to bring forth and nurture diverse life forms manifests the universe's first primordial bacteria within 320,000,000 years after each Big Birth. These bacteria are extremophiles and can survive in volcanic thermal vents as well as in outer space. Most planets, moons, and asteroids host primordial bacteria in their rocks that will bloom into a full spectrum of complex species given a suitable environment. The universe is teaming with life and we are all one family.

---

54 Image from: https://en.wikipedia.org/wiki/Evolution#/media/File:Ape_skeletons.png

In accordance with the law of causation, The Unitive Field fosters the evolution of synergistic life forms by interfacing with the protein activators in their DNA sequences. Every life organism is continually receiving feedback from its environment that mirrors back the energy it is projecting to nature. Those organisms that deplete nature or engage in relationships that are detrimental to other organisms will neither thrive nor long endure. Natural selection chooses those organisms that are most harmonious with their environment—those that enhance the wellbeing of nature and other life forms.

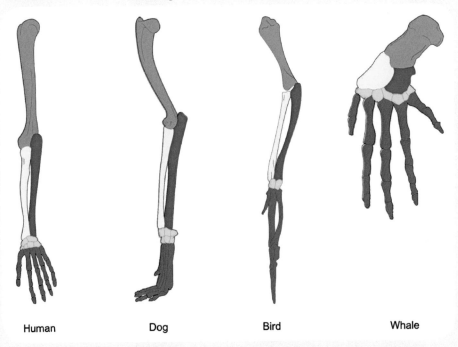

| Human | Dog | Bird | Whale |

Homologous bones in the limbs of tetrapods. The bones of these animals have the same basic structure, but have been adapted for specific uses.[55]

It is obvious by studying the bone structures above that nature is able to improvise to make many variations from a common design. This is an expression of the Unitive Field's causal intention of (c_i) 10^{144} Hreem to bring forth and nurture diverse life forms.

55 https://en.wikipedia.org/wiki/Evolution#/media/File:Homology_vertebratesen.svg

**The ancient Hawaiian wisdom of The Spirit of Aloha
is a guide for living in harmony with nature.**

Life forms thrive by living in harmony with the twelve organizing principles of the Unitive Field. The Spirit of Aloha eloquently expresses the universal wisdom of the Unitive Field's fundamental values. Unitive Field Theory chooses for its nomenclature the twelve Hawaiian terms comprising The Spirit of Aloha. To live life in The Spirit of Aloha is to understand Unitive Field Theory.

1. **Mahalo - Gratitude**: By looking at life experiences through the lens of appreciation, we realize that the entire Unitive Field is choreographing our present moment to offer us experiences that are perfect for our growth.

2. **Ha'aha'a - Humility**: By accepting the present moment of our lives, we open ourselves to allowing Unitive energy to flow through us.

3. **Ihi - Respect**: By seeing everything as a manifestation of the one Unitive Field, we naturally offer our love and service freely.

4. **Laulima - Simplicity**: By taking only what we need and living a life close to nature, we open to the wealth of being satisfied with what is given in the here and now and are freed from the delusion of always needing more to be happy.

5. **Ma'alahi - Cooperation**: By joyfully using our gifts and wealth to serve the Unitive Field through its creation, we allow the flow of Unitive energy to flow through us.

6. **Pono - Honesty**: By choosing a life of non-violence, we live in integrity with our true nature.

7. **Hauoli - Happiness**: By stilling our minds, we experience the peace within. This is the only joy that can truly fulfill our needs.

8. **Aloha - Love**: By allowing our joy to overflow in service to the Unitive Field in the form of its creation, we allow the breath of life to flow through us.

9. **Kuleana - Service**: By fulfilling our obligations to nature and our environment, by giving more than we consume, we live in harmony and balance.

10. **Noa - Freedom**: By choosing to depend on our connection with the Unitive Field as the source of our happiness, we free ourselves from depending on the approval of others.

11. **Maluhia - Peace**: By seeing all of our experiences as perfect for our ultimate growth, we live in appreciation, the seed of contentment.

12. **Lokahi - Unity**: By realizing our oneness with all of creation, we realize that we too are one with the Unitive Field.

"Ua Mau ke Ea o ka ʻĀina i ka Pono"

"Forever is Sustained, The Life of the Land by Righteousness"

This ancient Hawaiian wisdom is the essence of The Spirit of Aloha and the master key to understanding Unitive Field Theory.[56]

---

56 "Official Statehood Medal Commemorating the Admission of Hawaii as the 50th State." Licensed under fair use via Wikipedia. https://en.wikipedia.org/wiki/ File: Official_Statehood_Medal_Commemorating_the_ Admission_of_Hawaii_as_ the_50th_State.jpg

Nature is our ultimate Guru

Chapter 12

How Is Quantum Entanglement Used for Human Consciousness to Align with Unitive Consciousness?

ACCORDING TO UNITIVE Field Theory, the Big Bang (The Big Birth) is similar to a supernova. Just as a black hole is formed and remains after a supernova, so the universe has a core that remains in place after the Big Bang. That core is called the Bindhu. It is the place where the primordial Nada vibration abides in its sacred vibrational temple. It is the Godhead, the center of the universe, the source of the one consciousness of all beings. It is here that our awareness is experienced and our memories are stored. What we call the brain is simply a modem that is quantumly entangled with this one source of all consciousness that abides eternally within the Bindhu. The Bindhu is the gravitation hub of the universe. The universe as a whole rotates around the Bindhu every 12 billion years.

Because the entire universe is one living consciousness, every manifestation is part of this Unitive Consciousness. All localized consciousness that has name and form is one with Unitive Consciousness, although it is not the sum total of Unitive Consciousness. Though an ocean wave is one with the ocean, the wave is not the whole of the ocean.

As matter can transform into energy and energy can transform into matter, so consciousness can transform from localized consciousness into Unitive Consciousness. In fact, life's goal is for individual consciousness to achieve the state of Unitive Consciousness. To make this shift, the localized identity or ego needs to be transcended in order to experience Unitive Consciousness. This is the essential goal of the experience we call life.

When the mind is still, it becomes like a pristine lake reflecting
the bliss of our own consciousness.

The attainment of Unitive Consciousness is achieved by stilling the
mind so that the Unitive Consciousness, the source of all consciousness,
can be experienced without the distortion of localized consciousness
or thoughts. Just as the stars can only be seen in the absence of sunlight,
so the Unitive Consciousness can only be experienced in the absence of
localized consciousness or thoughts. In the silence of the mind, the
Nada is heard, and Unitive Consciousness is experienced.

There exists just one Unitive Field, manifesting as just one universe, that
eternally cycles between the state of being a singularity and the state of
being an expanded universe comprised of solar systems and galaxies.
The sum total of the universe's mass-energy, minus its negative force of
gravity, equals a grand total of zero. When all of the universe's positive
charges are added to all of the universe's negative charges, the grand total
of these charges is also zero.

Therefore, the Unitive Field is able to manifest the universe out of a quantity with no mass and no charge, using only the Law of Causation, $c_i^2 \, m = E$. The only unchanging reality in this manifested universe is consciousness itself, the organizing principle and source of all matter, energy, time, and space. The Unitive Field and all its spectrum of consciousness is all that truly exists. All manifestations of individual consciousness are simply rays of its color spectrum.

The universe's size and complexity are increasing with each universal cycle estimated to be 144 billion years from the big birth to the big reunion. The increase in complexity in nature and life forms is achieved by the lessons learned during each universal cycle. The lessons learned in the universe's university, which is called life, are remembered, and then the next big birth evolves in precision through the lessons learned from the previous universal cycles.

Life is the company that the Unitive Consciousness fosters to reflect its own loving energy. The Unitive Field bubbles in the bliss of its own love for its own foundational values within its singularity. Eventually, it digests the experiences of the last cosmic cycle and finishes its calculations for the next birth, and then, voilà!—another big birth. Each new birth yields a universe with greater complexity and synergies. The goal of the universal show is to create life forms, with localized consciousness, that can become aware of the Unitive Field so that the Unitive Field can have another way of understanding, "Who am I?" and "How may I serve?" Through life forms, the Unitive Field expresses its loving energy into the manifested creation, which is the body of the Unitive Field. The Unitive Field is ultimately one force field of love and service.

Life is the company that the Unitive Consciousness fosters to
reflect its own loving energy.

The state of alignment with Unitive Field energy is called yoga or union.
This Unitive state of consciousness is available to all life forms, and
the key to experiencing it is keeping the mind still by total surrender
of individual will to Unitive will. As long as we hold on to the idea that
the someone I am is separate from the Unitive Field, we will suffer by
experiencing the delusion of egoism. This misunderstanding is the
source of all misery and strife. In truth, we are one. There is no division
between any of us, or between us, and the Unitive Field itself. There
exists only one Unitive Field of consciousness, and we are all parts of
that field, and at the same time, one with the field itself. Just as a wave is
one with the ocean, at the same time, it is a wave. So we are one with the
field itself, even if we have localized consciousness.

Individual consciousness is just the reflection of Unitive Consciousness
on a mind. When the mind reflects Unitive Consciousness, it has the
experience of "I am." If it assumes "I am to be just the body and mind,"
the ignorance of egoism is born with its fleet of miseries.

A lightbulb is not illuminated with the effulgence of its own energy. It is empowered by an electrical source. The lightbulb is simply the channel through which the electrical energy is passing. It is the electrical energy that is actually animating the lightbulb. Similarly, the Unitive Consciousness is animating our consciousness. If we choose, we can align our consciousness with Unitive Consciousness to the point where Unitive Consciousness can automatically function through our consciousness. The result is dynamic productive service that enhances the wellbeing of nature. This state of yoga is the experience of being in the flow. It is productive dynamic activity that feels easeful, peaceful, and is useful.

The Unitive Field of consciousness pervades all six dimensions of the universe. This Unitive Consciousness creates life forms to use as mirrors for seeing itself. Its goal is to create life forms that evolve to experience Unitive Consciousness.

That way, the Unitive Field can see itself through that window.

It is a way that one energy field can divide itself into names and forms for the purpose of fulfilling its primary mission of knowing "Who am I?" and "How may I serve?" The Unitive Field expresses its love through service and the Unitive Field creates environments conducive for life forms that are synergistic with their environments.

Unitive Field Theory Nomenclature

To understand the nature of human consciousness, Unitive Field Theory draws its nomenclature from the ancient Vedic science of consciousness. The following Sanskrit terms are incorporated into Unitive Field Theory.

1. **Brahman:** The Unitive Consciousness that is the one eternal reality and the only unchanging aspect of the Unitive Field.

2. **Atman:** The Unitive soul with attributes and identity that reflect Brahman.

3. **Sat-Chid-Ananda:** Existence—Consciousness—Happiness. The eternal awareness of joy.

4. **Swaroop**: The true nature of the self of all beings, which is Satchidananda. It is the Brahman, the absolute consciousness, that is the unchanging Swaroop or nature and that gives rise to the Atman, the individual soul. Just as the wave is one with the ocean, yet has its own distinct form, so the Atman is a wave of consciousness within the ocean of Brahman. A wave has its own amplitude frequency and power, yet it is still one with the ocean and was never really separate from it.

   Vedic Assertion: Satchidananda Swaroop Ho Hum (Eternal existence, consciousness and bliss, my true nature is).

5. **Jivan**: The individual soul that can function in two ways or in a combination of both:

   a. Jivan as an ego: In this case, the Jivan identifies itself primarily with the mind and body and sees itself as separate from the Atman. This misidentification is the source of all misery, strife, war, and conflict. It is responsible for all that is called evil.

   b. Jivan as Jivan Muktan: In this liberated state, the Jivan realizes its Swaroop or true nature as being one with the Atman and is freed from the illusion that its consciousness is dependent on having a body and mind. It experiences Unitive Consciousness and realizes its oneness with all creation. It naturally and easefully expresses the values of the Unitive Consciousness, and its causal intentions (c_i) are effortlessly aligned with the Causal Intentions of the Unitive Field.

6. **Jnana**: The Conscience: The conscience is the umbilical cord connecting the Jivan with the Atman. The medium for the transmission of the Nada Hreem energy between Atman and the Jivan is through a wisdom channel known as Jnana or the conscience. This Jnana wisdom conscience channel is the key to understanding Unitive Field Theory.

The conscience is known by many names in different traditions such as: the way, the light, the truth, and the inner voice, morality, wisdom, prudence, fairness, mindfulness, the laws of nature, the word, the inner self, the reality, and the Tao. It is the way the consciousness of any life form determines it causal intentions (c_i), and knows which actions would be in alignment with the causal intentions of the Unitive Consciousness. Even animals have the innate wisdom of a conscious conscience. Innate to consciousness itself is Jnana, the ability to know how to use this consciousness in alignment with Unitive Consciousness. The Jnana wisdom is strengthened or weakened with each causal intention (c_i) that is executed by any being. The goal of life is to make choices of causal intentions that are in alignment with the wellbeing of nature. This strengthens the Jnana wisdom conscience channel.

Nature nurtures life forms whose causal intentions align with the Unitive Field's causal intention (c_i) of being serviceful.

The universe is a field of loving service. Any organism that aligns with that goal will prosper and thrive, and those that are not synergistic will not long endure. Thus natural selection that controls the evolution of all life forms is the outcome of the Law of Causation.

Because of the Law of Causation, every time a Jivan executes a causal intention (c_i), the resulting energy (E) will either strengthen or weaken its conscience's umbilical cord. Our entire life experience is determined by the thoughts and actions that we choose to entertain:

Thoughts reap actions,
Actions reap habits,
Habits reap character,
Character reaps destiny.

By entertaining thoughts that are in alignment with the Unitive Field causal intention (c_i), the Nada flow, which is the conscience, is strengthened. This results in greater health and insight being manifested.

The Unitive Field has the primary causal intention (c_i) to know "Who am I?" and "How may I serve?" In order to fulfill this intention, it prisms its one eternal consciousness into billions of color segments. This is similar to clear light refracting in a prism into a rainbow of colors. The sum total of all the colors of the rainbow still equals the original clear light, yet each color is an aspect of the clear light and adds a beauty and diversity to the Unitive Field.

The one Unitive Consciousness is the source of all mass-energy and consciousness in the universe, yet at the same time, it does not lose any of its own consciousness. This is accomplished in the same way that, in the presence of a powerful magnet, an iron bar will become magnetized. Yet the powerful magnet does not lose any of its own magnetic charge, even though it magnetizes countless other bars.

The consciousness of all beings have as their source
the One Unitive Consciousness that comprises
the first dimension of the Universe.

This same truth is expressed in the following ancient Sanskrit Vedic verse:

> Om Purnam-adah, Purnam idam,
> Purnat purnam-udatchyate.
> Purnasya purnam-adaya,
> Purnam-eva avasishyate.

> That is full, this also is full,
> This fullness came from that fullness.
> Though this fullness came from that fullness,
> That fullness remains forever full.

The universe and all of its consciousness is manifested out of the Unitive Consciousness. Yet the Unitive Consciousness remains full and is in no way diminished in the process.

The Unitive Field Game Plan

The Jivan is the Atman in individual consciousness.

The Jivan is given free will within certain limitations. Free will is another way of describing causal intention (c_i).

The Unitive Field assigns responsibility to each Jivan for the stewardship of its share of Hreem energy. This responsibility is assigned by the Law of Causation $c_i^2\, m = E$. The Jivan's causal intentions squared times the mass of those affected by those intentions is the resulting energy that the Jivan will be facing in its life experience.

The goal of the Jivan is to align with Unitive energy by performing actions that are synergistic with the environment and other organisms. Life is an opportunity to serve in helping creation evolve in alignment with the Causal Intention of the Unitive Field. The Unitive Field's primary causal intention is to be of service. That is the secret of the universe and of Unitive Field Theory. Live to serve and you will be aligned with the causal intention of Unitive Consciousness. That is the key to all wellbeing and to attaining the experience of the Jivan's oneness with the Atman.

The Unitive Field supports and empowers life forms that are synergistic with their environments and other organisms. Such a life form will thrive and prosper and be a branch to many species. Such is the evolution of species and the propagation of life forms that are in resonance with Unitive Field service and love energy within the dimensions of space and time.

Plant-Based Vegan Nutrition

The primary way humanity can be synergistic with the earth's ecosystem is for humanity to evolve to eating plant-based nutrition.

A reminder from Albert Einstein, "Nothing will benefit human health and increase the chances for survival of life on Earth as much as the evolution to a vegetarian diet.... Vegetarian food leaves a deep impression on our nature. If the whole world adopts vegetarianism, it can change the destiny of humankind."

This non-violent form of nutrition yields a causal intention that is harmonious and respectful to our fellow creatures and earth's environment.

This causal intention will then yield back to its source an energy that is aligned with the Unitive causal intention of fostering a diversity of life forms. Therefore, the Unitive energy will be able to flow through those life forms that are synergistic with their environments and enhancing the wellbeing of other life forms.

Moving to plant-based nutrition opens the door to allow the Unitive energy to flow through us. It is the single most important step any person can take to align with Unitive Consciousness.

Both Mahatma Gandhi and Albert Einstein were strong supporters of the Vegetarian Movement. They promoted plant-based nutrition as an expression of their pacifism and non-violent commitments.

Mahatma Gandhi addressing The London Vegetarian Society in 1931.[57]

Mahatma Gandhi joined the London Vegetarian Society's executive committee when he lived in London from 1888 to 1891. On November 20, 1931, during a visit to London for the second Round Table conference on India's future, he gave a speech to the society encouraging it to promote a meat-free diet as a matter of ethics, not health. Below is the opening passage from his speech:

Mr. Chairman, Fellow Vegetarians, and Friends,

When I received the invitation to be present at this meeting, I need not tell you how pleased I was because it revived old memories and recollections of pleasant friendships formed with vegetarians. I feel especially honoured to find on my right, Mr. Henry Salt. It was Mr. Salt's book *A Plea for Vegetarianism*, which showed me why apart from a hereditary habit, and apart from my adherence to a vow administered to me by my mother, it was right to be a vegetarian. He showed me why it was a moral duty incumbent on vegetarians not to live upon fellow-animals. It is, therefore, a matter of additional pleasure to me that I find Mr. Salt in our midst.

57 https://en.wikipedia.org/wiki/Veganism#/media/File:Gandhi_LVS_1931.jpg

Vegan nutrition is the optimal fuel for a human body. Humans are by nature herbivores. We have between thirty and forty feet of intestines. This clearly defines us as herbivores. When we eat plant-based nutrition, we can live healthy lives and be free from the many diseases caused by eating non-vegan foods.

Vegan nutrition is the most efficient way to eat. It takes less natural resources. Eating lower on the food chain is safer, as toxins become concentrated the higher one moves up the food chain.

It is kind to be merciful to animals. Because of the law of causation, the way humanity treats animals will be the way humanity's governments and corporations will treat humanity.

If humanity would move to plant-based nutrition, it would end the institution of war and create a more equal and just distribution of wealth within human societies.

Nature is a mirror. The way we treat nature is the way corporations and governments will treat us. There is no doubt about this. History shows this clearly.

If we live in harmony with nature by offering animals the respect they deserve, then nature will bless us with a life of fulfillment. If we harm animals, nature will be forced to reflect back to us the experience of suffering. The choice is ours, and the vote is made with each bite of food that we take. Transform your life and the life of the planet by choosing wisely.

Choose plant-based nutrition and nature will bless you.

The Vegan Food Groups

Fruits • Vegetables • Legumes (Beans)
Whole Grains • Seeds • Nuts

Fruits and vegetables are the "Mana" from heaven provided by
the Unitive Field for Humanity.

The cornucopia of Fruits blesses humanity with a great variety
of delicious, nutritious, and colorful treats.

Roots provide delicious and
nutritious sources of sustained
energy for humanity

Falafel is a Vegan Middle Eastern
staple food that has nourished
humanity for over 5 millennia

Stir-fried veggies are a delight

Vegan Pizza is delicious and easy
to digest

Fruit Salad feeds the body and
the soul

Rice and beans form a complete
vegan protein

Vegan cheeses are delicious, nutritious and easy to digest.

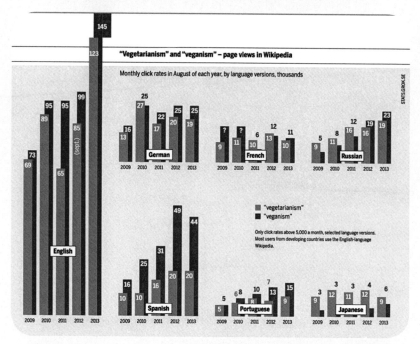

Vegans form one the fasting growing segments of humanity. Vegans are the wave of the future and the dawn of a human race that harmonizes with its environment.[58]

58 https://en.wikipedia.org/wiki/Veganism#/media/File:Vegetarianism_and_
veganism_page_views,_Wikipedia.jpg

The Veggie Pride Parade in Lower Manhattan
is an annual celebration of Vegan and Vegetarian diets.

„Die stärksten Tiere
sind Pflanzenfresser:
Gorillas, Büffel,
Elefanten und Ich."

PFLANZEN
FRESSER

Patrik Baboumian
„Stärkster Mann Deutschlands" **PeTA**
stoppt tierquälerei!

Patrik Baboumian, Germany's Strongest Man is a Vegan.[59]

Vegan nutrition is ideal for bodybuilders and athletes. Many of the world's greatest athletes are Vegan.[60]

---

59 http://www.peta.de/baboumian#.VipAYPmrSUk
60 http://www.greatveganathletes.com/vegan_athlete_patrik-baboumian-vegan-strongman

The Eight Limbs of Yoga are the basis of Unitive Field Theory

The Eight Limbs of Ashtanga Yoga are a Tree of Life
to those who take shelter in its branches.

Unitive Field Theory is based on the science of Ashtanga Yoga. The science of yoga has a history that spans more than five millennium. The Ashtanga Yoga or eight limbs of yoga are a scientific method for the evolution from individual consciousness to Unitive Consciousness.

The Yamas and Niyama are a compass guiding us to true integrity.

1. **Yamas:**

   > **Ahimsa:** Nonviolence
   > **Satya:** Truthfulness
   > **Asteya:** Non-stealing
   > **Brahmacharya:** Celibacy, moderation, faithfulness
   >   to one's partner
   > **Aparigraha:** Non-greed

2. **Niyamas:**

   > **Saucha:** Purity of mind, speech, and body
   > **Santosha:** Contentment
   > **Tapas:** Perseverance in the face of obstacles
   > **Swadhyaya:** Spiritual study
   > **Ishwarapranidhana:** Surrender to Unitive Consciousness

   The Yamas and Niyamas are an eloquent expression of the twelve foundational qualities of the Unitive Field. By observing the Yamas and Niyamas, the causal intention of the Jivan is aligned with Unitive causal intention.

3. **Asana:** The practice of the yoga poses that vitalize and tone the body and mind.

4. **Pranayama:** The breathing practices that invigorate and calm the body and mind.

5. **Pratyahara:** Sense withdrawal. The skill of experiencing the here and now moment without the experience of thoughts.

6. **Dharana:** The practice of making the mind one-pointed. The practice of meditation.

7. **Dyana:** The experience of the stilled mind.

8. **Samadhi:** The experience of the balanced state of oneness with Unitive Consciousness.

These eight limbs of yoga are also known as raja yoga or the royal path. They are a scientific progression that leads the Jivan from egoism to Unitive Consciousness.

The Science of Nada Meditation: The Sacred Sound of Silence

When you sit in silence, you can hear a ringing sound in your ears. Nada Meditation uses your inner ringing sounds to help you attain Unitive consciousness.

Ancient Tibetan temple chimes depict the sacred tones of the Nada.

By meditating on the sacred Nada vibration, we can still the mind and tune into a deeper level of consciousness. We experience the "Inner-Net" and open the channel for the wisdom of "Unitive Field Direct-Drive" to flow through us. This experience is easeful, peaceful, and dynamically useful. It is similar to a computer connecting to the Internet and accessing its vast wisdom, instead of just continually rummaging through its own limited files.

The experience of complete silence is impossible, for woven into the fabric of consciousness is the high pitched hum of the Nada. This is the sacred Om vibration that is the very source of the one eternal consciousness of which all life forms are cells. The Nada is the source of the "I am" and of its intention, "How may I serve?" All consciousness will have this inner hum. Even when one leaves the body at the time of transition, commonly referred to as death, the Nada hum continues as the eternal consciousness transitions to its new home. In this universe of constant change, the Nada hum is the only absolute unchanging reality. It exists even within the primal singularity and is the organizing principle of the Universe itself and of all the cells of consciousness that are called life forms.

All consciousness is One with Unitive consciousness and is eternal. When a sound system is turned on, it has a base hum even before the music begins to play. So all consciousness has the Nada hum. The Nada is the sound of silence.

The Nada is also the most healing sound that the mind can experience. It is the sound that tunes all the cells of the brain to harmonize with each other. It is similar to when the conductor of an orchestra strikes a tone to which all the musicians tune their instruments. That way, they all harmonize with each other. The Nada is the tone that harmonizes all of the neurons of the brain.

In the Yoga Sutras of Patanjali, the goal of Yoga is summarized in the second Sutra, "Yoga's Chitta Vritti Nirodhah." This means Yoga or union occurs when the waves of the mind are stilled.

The practice of stilling the thoughts of the mind and focusing the consciousness of the mind on the Nada is referred to as Dyana, or meditation. It is the seventh rung of Ashtanga Yoga. Regular meditation on the sacred Nada vibration transforms the brain into a channel through which Unitive Consciousness can flow through us in "Direct-Drive." This is the state of Samadhi, the eighth rung of Ashtanga Yoga, and it is the experience of Oneness with Unitive consciousness. This is the goal of life and the greatest gift any person can offer in service to humanity.

The word Tinnitus is from the Latin Tinnīre which means "to ring." Tinnitus is the hearing of sound when no external sound is present. In Sanskrit, the Nada vibration is described as "Anahata": the sound that is made without anything striking, or the sound of silence.

Learn to experience and embrace your inner orchestra. Try to spend some time each day in stilling the mind and focusing on the Nada. During these times, train the mind gently. Learn to incorporate the Nada into your daily life, for instance when you are cleaning your home, making meals, walking or whenever the mind isn't needed, give it a safe place to reside.

The sacred Nada vibration is the birthright of all humanity and the sweetest gift of the Unitive Field to its beloved life forms. Nada meditation melts the ego's illusion of separateness.

Investing fifteen minutes in the morning and fifteen minutes before going to sleep will bear sweet fruit in a short time. Regular meditation can transform our lives so that we work more efficiently and avoid accidents. Nada meditation is the greatest gift we can offer ourselves and the world.

The Lotus is the symbol of the Spiritual Path. Although it grows
in the stagnant muddy water, it rises above that and is pristine.

The following ancient Sanskrit sloka expresses the 10^{144} Hreem force of
intention for the Unitive Field to nurture life in the universe:

> Om Sarveshaam Svastir-Bhavatu
> Sarveshaam Shaantir-Bhavatu
> Sarveshaam Purnnam-Bhavatu
> Sarveshaam Manggalam-Bhavatu
> Om Shaantih Shaantih Shaantih
>
> May there be Wellbeing everywhere,
> May there be Peace everywhere
> May there be Fulfillment everywhere
> May there be Auspiciousness everywhere,
> Om Peace, Peace, Peace, be unto all.

Unified Field Theory Summary

THERE EXISTS A sacred vibration that was formed by density variations in the primordial field of nothingness. It is composed of six pairs of fundamental values. This sacred vibration is created by the attraction of each value to the next value in the chain. The cycle repeats eternally and is the only unchanging factor in creation. This vibration is referred to as The Bindhu, The Field, The Word, The Nada, The Lord God, Om, The Unitive Consciousness, and many other sacred names. This vibration gives rise to the conscious experience of "I am." The "I am" consciousness gives rise to the intention, "How may I serve?" The Unitive Consciousness is like clear light; the consciousness of life forms is the Unitive Consciousness refraction in nature, its color spectrum.

When all the colors in its spectrum are added together again, they equal clear light.

Gratitude – Humility
Respect – Simplicity
Cooperation – Honesty
Happiness – Love
Service – Freedom
Peace – Unity

There exists in nature just one universe. It is a six-dimensional screen upon which is projected the one Unitive Consciousness that is its essence. The screen is called the Unitive Field. It is eternal, yet it is continually evolving. The Unitive Field has defined proportions, with its edges folding back into itself. There is, by definition, nothing outside of itself.

Approximately 95.1 percent of the mass-energy within the Unitive Field is formed of Dark Matter and Dark Energy. These form the skeletal and muscular systems of the living organism that is the universe. They are not withdrawn back into the singularity during the Big Reunion. Rather, they continue to rotate around the Bindhu every 12 billion years.

Additionally, within the Unitive Field is approximately 4.9 percent fluctuating matter-energy that forms the observable universe. The observable universe is made up of atomic elements that form gases, dust, asteroids, planets, stars, nebulas, black holes, and galaxies. The universe offers nurturing environments for life forms to develop and thrive. The conscious awareness of these life forms is one with the one Unitive Consciousness of the universe. Just like blood that is pumped out of the heart eventually returns back to the heart, so the observable universe is pumped out of the Bindhu only to return 144 billion years later.

On the quantum or subatomic level, all energy in the Unitive Field is made from one primal energy called Hreem. Hreem is produced by the Unitive Field within its primordial Singularity by the Law of Causation: $c_i^2 \, m = E$. This equation defines the relationship between the cause and effect of any action. Every action in the universe has as its source a causal intention (ci), which squared and multiplied by the mass of those affected by the action (m), equals the energy returned to the causal intention (E). This is known as The Golden Rule or The Law of Karma.

The primordial singularity is the seed of the universe. At the moment of the Big Birth, a precise quantity of its Hreem energy is transposed into the universe's most basic subatomic particle, Hreemium. In a finely tuned birth, it expands into the observable universe. The Unitive Consciousness carefully choreographs the universe's unfoldment to create stable environments for life to flourish.

The four forces of nature are all manifestations of just one force, electromagnetism. All electromagnetic waves travel at the speed of light and form the brainwaves of the Unitive Consciousness. It is through these electromagnetic waves that the Unitive Consciousness creates order in the universe and provides stable environments for life to flourish.

The Big Birth is similar to a Supernova and leaves behind a super-dense core called The Bindhu. The Bindhu is the gravitational hub of the universe. The universe as a whole rotates around the Bindhu every 12 billion years.

Within the Bindhu is contained the holy of holies, the one Unitive Consciousness that is the source of the universe. It never changes, although in it presence the entire universe eternally dances. The Unitive Consciousness is connected by quantum entanglement to all life forms in the universe. All awareness in the universe happens within the Bindhu. Your awareness of these words at this moment is located in the Bindhu. Free will or causal intention (ci) is given for the Jivan to freely surrender its ego in service to the Unitive Consciousness by aligning with its twelve fundamental values. To the degree that the Jivan makes this alignment, the Unitive Consciousness is able to add its support. The Unitive Field nurtures its abundant life forms and interacts with the protein activators in their DNA sequences to foster their development. All life in the universe derives from one primordial extremophile bacteria that began within the first 320 million years after the Big Birth. All life in the universe share at least 6 percent of the same DNA. All life is literally one family.

Ultimately, the 4.9 percent that comprises the observable universe is withdrawn back into the Bindhu. Each life cycle of the universe lasts for approximately 144 billion years. We are approximately 13.8 billion years into our current universal incarnation. This universal life cycle is eternal. With each cycle, the Unitive Field fosters life in ever-evolving complexity, diversity, and consciousness. The goal of the universal cycle is to create life forms that experience oneness with Unitive Consciousness. The universe is the expression of the creative love energy of the Unitive Consciousness whose intentions are to know who am I, and how may I serve. Life is the mirror through which the Unitive Consciousness sees itself and expresses its loving energy.

Oceans are fields of consciousness and are
the mothers of Life.

About the Author

Fredrick Swaroop Honig, aka Swami Swaroopananda, is a Nature Guardian. He is a leading exponent of Plant-Based Nutrition and of Nada Yoga, the science of meditation.

SWAROOP WAS ORDAINED as a Monk in the Holy Order of Sannyas and as a Minister of Integral Yoga in 1977 by the acclaimed Integral Yoga founder and interfaith leader, Sri Swami Satchidananda, who was ordained in 1949 by the renowned Sri Swami Sivananda, founder of The Divine Life Society.

For twenty years, starting at age twenty-one, Swaroop lived, studied, taught, and served as a monastic member of Satchidananda Ashrams and Integral Yoga Institutes. He also offered his popular yoga, meditation, and stress management courses at universities and international retreat centers. During this period, Swaroop played key roles in organizing interfaith programs and in the design and construction of The Light Of Truth Universal Shrine, "LOTUS."

Since 1994, Swaroop has served in the foundation of The Spirit of Aloha Temple, Botanical Gardens and Bird Sanctuary on the north shore of Maui. The Gardens are dedicated to living in harmony with nature, through alignment with its twelve organizing principles. The Gardens are a living classroom for traditional Hawaiian organic horticulture and delicious plant-based nutrition. To tour The Gardens is to experience a heaven on earth and a deeper appreciation and understanding of nature.

Mahalo Nui Loa

For more information or to arrange a visit or program, we invite you to visit us online at www.SpiritofAloha.org.

Made in the USA
Lexington, KY
13 November 2018